TRILOGY
CHRISTIAN
PUBLISHING

The
REVELATION
Of
JESUS

David Binion
with Max Davis

TRILOGY
CHRISTIAN
PUBLISHING

TRILOGY
CHRISTIAN
PUBLISHING

Trilogy Christian Publishers
A Wholly Owned Subsidary of Trinity Broadcasting Network
2442 Michelle Drive
Tustin, CA 92780

Design, Diane Whisner
Cover image, Getty Images. Photographer, Peter Cade

Library of Congress Cataloging-in-Publication Data is available.

ISBN 978-1-68556-520-6
ISBN 978-1-68556-521-3 (ebook)

The
REVELATION
Of
JESUS

For two years I have watched my husband immerse himself in the Book of Revelation. Since that morning in May of 2020 when he woke up and shared with me that God had spoken to him to "write the Revelation of Jesus," I have watched his faithfulness to this divine assignment. He started penning songs first; he was faithful to the scripture — not adding to, nor taking away. He began planning for a worship album devoted to these songs. And then, he began writing the book you're holding in your hands: The Revelation of Jesus, An Unexpected Love Story. All for the glory of Jesus, all so that we may see Jesus revealed as our Conquering King, worthy of our lives laid down in worship and service to Him. As you read may you receive the blessing from Revelation 1:3, "Blessed is the one who reads aloud the words of this prophecy, and blessed are those who hear, and who keep what is written in it…"

Nicole Binion
Worship Artist and Lead Pastor
Dwell Church, Allen, Texas

The revelation of Jesus — a powerful manuscript — written through the lens of worship, and crafted in a way that only a hungry disciple of Christ could ever bring. For years, the book of Revelation intimidated me. When I finally found the courage to step into its pages, I found JESUS revealed in and through every chapter, and eventually, the words *Come Up Here* from Revelation 4 became the bedrock and framework for my own journey of leading others in worship.

Thankyou David for plumbing the depths and answering the call to bring fresh insight to this powerful book, helping others like me who needed someone to walk them through the mysteries, the warnings, and the great love of God dripping from every page.

From a grateful heart,
Darlene Zschech

David Binion has written a fascinating study of Revelation from the perspective of a seasoned worship leader. He retells the story of John on Patmos and adds to it a wealth of personal experiences of the Holy Spirit. And the bonus is a whole collection of tailor-made worship songs based on the main themes of Revelation. This isn't a commentary, and it doesn't set out to answer all your questions, but I think David has caught something of the heart and experience of John and this book will undoubtedly bring you closer to the heartbeat of God as John encountered it.

David Campbell
Professor TheosUniversity
Author of *Mystery Explained: A Simple Guide to Revelation.*

If you could take the gifts of a seer, a gifted musician, a poet, a wordsmith, and a passionate God-chaser and wrap them in an individual, you would have a David Binion. In his book, The Revelation of Jesus, he moves us past the common predilection to only see monsters to see the real truth: Worship is warfare! David's insights remind me of a famous quote by G. K. Chesterton. "Fairy tales do not tell children dragons exist. Children already know dragons exist. Fairy tales tell children the dragons can be killed." In real life, I have seen David's remarkable ability to lead thousands into the Presence of God in an atmosphere of worship through his skillful use of word pictures, Spirit-energized music, and the mixture of "new and old." His book, filled with personal testimonies of God encounters, will motivate you to see God's victorious intentions in His divine plan for His people.

Bishop Joseph L. Garlington, Sr.
Founding Pastor of Covenant Church of Pittsburgh
Presiding Bishop of Reconciliation! An International Network of Churches and Ministries

David Binion, to his core, is a worshipper, as is his wife Nicole, as are their children. Having had the privilege of knowing David and Nicole and the family for many years I have observed at a distance and up close their journey in Christ, and the impact and influence God has granted them all around the world. There is a profound reason for that. As worshippers, their heart is for intimacy with the Triune God. It flows out of every lyric they write and every song they sing. David takes you places in his words and the melodies he carries them on. He is named after the Sweet Psalmist of Israel, and whether or not his dad and mom realized how prophetic they were in naming him after David, he would indeed lay hold of "harps and bowls" in the spirit of David the Beloved King and lead us in procession before the Throne of God. When David began to write the songs for what you now hold in your hand as this book, I was deeply moved by the verses and the melodies he shared with me. One thing I would contend above all else is that the Revelation of John, which is the unveiling of Jesus, has one goal in mind: pure spiritual worship! David intends in writing these pages to take us toward that desired outcome of worship, precisely because of the Testimony of Jesus, which indeed is the Spirit of Prophecy. Follow David as he leads you in worshipful reverence, line by line. Soak it in and let it do for you what happened to John the Revelator as he beheld the unveiling of the ineffable Christ: let it catch you up and carry you away in the Spirit, immerse you in the worship of Jesus, and cause you to bow before the Father and lay down your crown in recognition of his glorious Kingdom.

Bishop Mark J. Chironna
Church On The Living Edge
Mark Chironna Ministries

ॐ

Wow! If you want your eyes to be opened, then The Revelation of Jesus is for you. It will open many eyes to the wondrous love, will, and return of Jesus. Thank you, David, for opening my eyes and reminding me what time it is. I love you brother and I love this much-needed book!

Cece Winans
Your friend and sister

৯৹

Theologians have for centuries labored to unlock the profound mysteries that rest quietly beneath the surface of what we now recognize as the book of Revelations or what John was divinely inspired to call The Revelation of Jesus!

While religion has relegated much of John's writings from the Prison of Patmos to the unfolding of future events or those of the distant past.

My dear friend David Lee Binion dares to capture the eternal essence of John's words and translate them into a language that makes them relevant to all who welcome the unparalleled Spiritual outpouring that is now upon us!

In his new book, *The Revelation of Jesus* David successfully makes the book of Revelations come to life in the Here and NOW.

David's prophetic encounters of the eternal kind, drawn from his life experience as a seasoned presence-driven praise and worship leader, more than qualify him to write on such a timely subject as this.

Lastly, anyone who's shared the privilege of being in one of David and his family's praise and worship gatherings will tell you; that as he, his wife Nicole, and gifted daughter Madison open their hearts to sing, JESUS COMES; bringing with Him the sound of Heaven and all that it offers for the thirty of soul!

As you read the life-changing truths metaphors and principles embedded in each of David's faith-infused chapters you will be inspired charged and challenged to welcome Celebrate and entertain the unparalleled Spiritual out-powering that only comes with a TRUE Revelation Of Jesus! May David's words grant you a fresh new level of unrestricted access to.

Bishop Mark Steven Filkey
Senior Pastor and Founder
West Coast World Outreach Church, Stockton, California

❧

No one can lead you into an encounter with God in worship like my friend David can.

Exploring the prophetic parts of Revelation takes extensive Bible study and insight. Writing songs about the Book of Revelation takes even more skill and ability. David has done both!

The Revelation of Jesus is a collection of songs, bible history, and a power ful revelation that will take you into the presence of God from page 1.

If you are hungry for a fresh encounter with Jesus and desire a greater understanding of the Book of Revelation, then don't miss this book!

Martha Munizzi
Renown Worship Artist and Lead Pastor
Epic Life Church, Orlando, Florida

❧

The very word Revelation means to "reveal" and that's exactly what David's book has done. In a time where living in the shallows of our spiritual understanding is popular, this book takes us where we MUST go as Christians….to the true revelation of who Jesus is and what is to come. Very few books on the subject of Revelation appeals to everyone but this book does. It's a must-read. The reader will get the most beautiful glimpse into who Jesus is by not only getting to know Him but actually "seeing Him". David, you did it. The church and every Christian need this book now more than ever.

Mary Alessi
Worship Pastor

Metro Life Church, Miami, Florida In his book, *The Revelation Of Jesus,* David Binion masterfully draws us into the presence of the Lord, just as he does when he leads people into worship. It's as though the typewriter became his keyboard and with every stroke of every sentence my heart started beating because I knew His Presence had entered the room. In an exquisite depiction, he places us on the island of Patmos exiled but like John, we know we are not alone. Your faith will arise to a new level, knowing whatever your circumstance, you too can enter into the spirit realm and receive a revelation from heaven that will draw you closer to Him.

Maria Durso
Saints Church

෪

In his timely book, *The Revelation Of Jesus*, David Binion allows us a rare peek into a complex mystery. While reading this book, its as though divine hands pull us onto the island of Patmos, where John is exiled and into the presence of the Lord and His Presence becomes a tangible reality. With every sentence, David Binion stirs within us a fresh desire for true revival in our own personal life and also a deep longing to see it take place on the earth knowing that He is coming soon. As we focus our eyes on Him and posture our heart toward Him we are propelled to press through regardless of where we find ourselves knowing that if God could speak to John in isolation, He can speak to us.

Pastor Michael Durso
Overseer Saints Church

CONTENTS

I am so grateful to so many who helped make this project possible.

First of all, I want to say thanks to Max Davis who helped me write this book. Not only have I discovered a great collaborator but a new friendship that I will cherish forever. What's next? Let's write another one!

To David Campbell, whose writing helped bring great insight in my study of the last book of the Bible. Thank you sir for your great wisdom.

To my oversight pastor, and great friend, Bishop Joseph Garlington. Your love and guidance over the last several years have become so life-giving to me.

To Mitch Wong, my newest songwriting partner, you were Heaven sent. Your friendship is my great treasure. Before this book was even considered, the idea to write the songs was born in a conversation. I shared with you my encounter with the Lord, and you immediately embraced the vision. Your gift is unparalleled.

To the other songwriters, Steffany Gretzinger, Dwan Hill, Krissy Nordhoff, and my beautiful daughter Madison Grace Binion. Thanks for helping me dive deep into these scripture songs.

To my Dwell Church family, thanks for letting me experiment with each chapter as we journeyed through the book of Revelation for almost a year.

To my wife and ministry partner, Nicole Binion, thank you for letting me immerse myself in this project and write for months at a time while navigating our travel schedule and pastoring our church. I love you more and more.

To my oldest son, Denver Cole Binion, and his beautiful wife Ana, you guys have served so well helping us manage ministry life, as well as watching over Carson David when the schedule got so crazy.

And of course, to Carson David Binion, you have shown us that a child with special needs can open our eyes to see that impossibilities can be shattered and dreams can still come true. You are a beautiful gift.

And finally, to Matt and Laurie Crouch, thank you for believing in us and sharing the vision of our hearts to fully see The Revelation of Jesus.

This book is not meant to be a complete verse-by-verse commentary or textbook. It simply takes a look at the Book of Revelation through a slightly different lens, offering a fresh view. I've done the religious thing and have come to a point in my life where nothing is more important to me than intimacy with Jesus and living in His presence. It's out of that place of intimacy with Him that everything else flows and is the lifeblood of everything I do. As a worship leader, songwriter, and pastor I love being drawn into His presence, and I love drawing others into that place with Him. But what does all that have to do with the Book of Revelation? I've discovered that as much as the book is about end times, it's also about worship and intimacy with Jesus. As you will see, it is a love story. A few friends helped me write the songs that go along with what we have discovered on our journey through this life-altering book of the Bible.

When I say different lens, I'm not talking about new revelation outside of Scripture or reinterpreting solid exegesis. I'm talking about fresh illumination, just a slightly different view from the typical end-time prophecy book. So, grab your Bible and bags and journey through this final book of the Bible with us. And get ready to be drawn into His presence and worship!

An added note: For easy reading flow, Revelation scripture references are documented in the text at the end of the scripture. All other scripture references are footnoted.

For Chapters 1–6, read Revelation 1–3.

For Chapters 7–10, read Revelation 4–8.

For Chapters 11–12, read Revelation 9–14.

For Chapters 13–16, read Revelation 15–19.

For Chapters 7–19, read Revelation 20–22.

Acknowledgments

A project such as this would never be birthed without the help of many selfless and gifted people.

I'm grateful for author Darrell Johnson and his book *Discipleship on the Edge*. It greatly enhanced my understanding of the Book of Revelation. I'm also grateful for the in-depth conversations I was able to share with Bishop Mark Chirrona and Phil Munsey, whose understanding of this subject matter is stunning.

It's not often I personally experience a liberating paradigm shift in my theology, but I've experienced just that with this book and album project. I'll explain more about my new perspective in a moment, but first it's important to understand where my paradigm was with respect to the often-misunderstood book of Revelation.

Like many of you, the book of Revelation intimidated and confused me more than any other book in the Bible. Although a necessary part of through the Bible reading, I'll admit I never looked forward to it. Alright, if I'm being completely transparent with you, I dreaded it.

Countless theologians over the centuries have written extensive works attempting to dissect it, intellectualize it, and even predict future events based on it. Still, many of us resist reading even the few worthwhile expositions or even reading the seemingly foreboding book itself.

I'm not suggesting that the end of time as we know it isn't going to be just as challenging as Revelation insists it will be. I'm also not suggesting that there are not prophetic events foretold in it that will inevitably unfold as they are written — we may be closer to some of them than we like to think. But the doom and gloom we tend to read at cringeworthy, face value is not the only theme of the story.

Having run a Christian film company for decades before assuming leadership at TBN, I find myself digging for the story behind the story when I read a book or a script. And in this case, the compelling story behind the story of Revelation turns out to be the undeniable, unrivaled holiness and glory of our victorious Savior!

Imagine, if during our formative years as followers of Jesus, we were inspired to see Revelation as a book of victory, awe, and worship, rather than a fear inspiring book of trials and tribulations — which will tragically be the case for those unfortunate souls who reject the loving Savior. (Anyone on the fence about accepting Christ as Savior should read Revelation for that cautionary reason.)

A refreshing understanding of being divinely inspired to worship by the book of Revelation is exactly where David Binion ended up through a series of eye-opening events in his life as you'll read. And it's exactly where I've ended up as well.

For years I knew I would experience a paradigm shift along this line would occur in my life. It was over a decade ago that I heard the still, small voice of the Lord speak into my spirit that one day that I would experience "a reset" in my understanding about the book of Revelation. And I'm excited to say, that day has finally come through this project. In fact, to say that I've simply experienced "a reset" in my thinking might be an understatement.

It's nothing short of spiritually liberating for me to read the book of Revelation now with a spirit of awe and worship. I look forward with great anticipation to reading the book I once dreaded and come away from it elevated, realizing anew with each chapter just how awesome and all-powerful the God we serve truly is! Even the angels are endlessly awestruck by His glory as they sing, "Holy, Holy, Holy is the Lamb that was slain…"

I've known David Binion for about as long as I can remember. He and his sister sang on TBN as kids. Today, as a pastor and gifted worship leader, David has proven over the years that he's an authentic lover of Jesus who lives to glorify God through all he does. So, naturally, when he approached me in the Spring of 2021 telling me he was prompted to "write the revelation of Jesus" I was instantly and completely onboard with this very worthwhile and timely project.

Like me, once you hear his heartfelt songs of worship, chapter by chapter, and read his refreshing, paradigm-shifting companion book, you will never again be intimidated or frightened by this awesome book of the Revelation (of Jesus).

—Matthew Crouch

1

The Voice

Blessed is the one who reads aloud the words of this prophecy,
and blessed are those who hear it and take to heart what is written in it,
because the time is near.

Revelation 1:3 NIV

The Book of Revelation.

Just reading those words evokes an array of images ranging from late-night prophets of doom and gloom broadcasting their end-time predictions across the staticky AM airwaves, to multi-degreed experts with charts, detailed and colorful but always a bit confusing. Every expert has a chart . . . and a book with the latest insight and secret. Now don't get me wrong. I'm all for colorful charts and books with insights and secrets, and I believe in end-time prophecy. It's just that all of it gets a bit overwhelming at times—the wars, beasts, plagues, blood (lots of blood), locusts with stinging tails, smoke, fire, thunder and lightning, bowls that pour out death and judgment . . . To many, the Book of Revelation is a frightening tale they would just as soon skip altogether.

To be fair, though, there are wonderful images in the Book of Revelation too. Glorious angels and creatures with magnificent faces worshiping around God's throne, the seven Spirits of God, elders casting down their crowns, horsemen riding celestial steeds, a crystal river flowing through the heavenly city built with foundations of precious jewels, streets of gold, mansions, the Tree of Life, and giant gates made of solid pearl. Oh yeah, there's no need for the

sun or moon because the light of God shines there! Sounds like a
pretty amazing place that I can't wait to call home one day. When
Paul was caught up to Paradise, he said he saw and "heard things
so astounding that they cannot be expressed in words, things no
human is allowed to tell."[1] No doubt heaven is going to be incredible
beyond human imagination, and it is our ultimate home. That's
why Paul also instructed us to set our minds on "things above, not
on things on the earth."[2] The problem is, we live on earth in this
present time-based continuum, a God-created opening in eternity,
and have to deal with problems like work pressures, rising gas
prices, Covid-19, aging bodies, did Johnny miss his bus, and who's
bringing the turkey this year? We've all heard the saying, "Don't
be so heavenly minded that you're no earthly good." That's not
from Scripture, but there is an element of truth in it. Heaven is our
eternal home, yes, but God did put us on this earth for a purpose.
Personally, I want to fulfill that purpose and then go home. I
love what is written in the Book of Acts about David fulfilling his
purpose. It says: "Now when David had served God's purpose in his
own generation, he fell asleep."[3] I love that, and that's what I want
for myself. I want to accomplish my assignment *in my generation,* fall
asleep, and wake up in heaven. Let's face it: most of us look forward
to heaven one day, but we're not really in a rush to get there. And
even though Paul tells us that being absent from the body means
being present with the Lord[4], we don't want to leave our loved ones
and tend to keep a tight grip on this world. I'm just being real. So,
though the Book of Revelation intrigues us, for many it takes a
backseat to the pressures and purposes of the now. We tend to focus
on the parts of the Bible that help us have victory in our lives here.

---

1   2 Corinthians 12:4 NLT
2   Colossians 3:2 NKJV
3   Acts 13:36 (NIV)
4   2 Corinthians 5:8

While we don't want to be so heavenly minded that we aren't any good, we'd do well to heed Pastor Bill Johnson's contrasting thought: "Unless you become heavenly minded, you'll be no earthly good."

As a kid who grew up in the church as the son of a healing evangelist, I saw some pretty amazing things that could only be explained as God. They impacted my life forever. My dad and mom knew how to shake heaven. I'd be playing with my toy trucks in the hallway of our old home and bump up against their bedroom door and hear the roar of prayer. I'd keep on playing, but hearing your folks *pray* like that sure makes an imprint on a kid. I once saw a tumor disappear off a lady's neck. The thing was the size of a baseball, and when my dad prayed, it just started shrinking, then *poof*, it was gone, vanished. I've seen blind eyes opened; terminal cancer healed overnight; even a woman raised from the dead. Really, actually dead. Saw it with my own eyes.

Yes, I know the reality and power of God well. Yet when it came to the Book of Revelation, for years I would read right through it, kind of afraid of it because of all the dark chapters and not really grasping the heavenly parts. I'd think, *One day I'll understand, but for now just give me something I can apply to my life, like John, Ephesians, Romans, or Hebrews.* Of course, I read the Left Behind book series along with 20 million other good church kids. That helped me get some of the concepts of Revelation, but there are so many ideas and opinions in so many books about what the Book of Revelation really means. Honestly, I could never fully wrap my mind around this wonderfully frightening book, and I think a lot of us feel the same.

One thing is for sure: God is real to me. He's alive and fully present. Since those early years when He came into my heart, Jesus has continued to draw me into more of Himself. I'm a lover of the One who first loved me and died for me to make a way where there was no way. I owe everything to Him. Knowing and worshiping Jesus is my heart and my life. Take Him out of the equation and there is no reason to live. Leading people into His presence through worship is what I do. One aspect of worship is an intimate, divine dance between the Creator and His creation. As a worship leader my calling is to draw people into that dance. We will dig deeper into that later. But how do we dance with God? We are flawed and sinful creatures, and God is infinite and powerful and holy. God told Moses, "You cannot see My face, for no one sees me and lives."[5] If we can't see God's face and live, how can we dance and be intimate with Him? You can't dance intimately with someone without gazing into their eyes and seeing their face. The answer is Jesus. When we are intimate with Jesus and our spirit is intertwined with His through the Holy Spirit inside us, we are intimate with God. When we dance with Jesus, we are dancing with God. After all, Paul wrote that Jesus "is the *image* of the invisible God."[6] The writer of Hebrews said, "The Son is the radiance of God's glory and the *exact representation* of His being."[7] If you want to know what God is like, look at Jesus. If you want intimacy with God, dance with Jesus. That's what I was doing. Living my life, keeping my eyes fixed on Him, worshiping Him. The Book of Revelation was just something tacked on. I had to read it, but I didn't have to understand it. I wasn't taping verses from Revelation to my desk lamp.

Then IT happened.

The Voice.

A divine encounter.

It wasn't a dream. It was a voice, vibrating, shaking me out of a dead sleep. I awoke to the sound of a voice, deep but gentle, strong

---

5   Exodus 33:20 NIV
6   Colossians 1:15 NIV, emphasis added
7   Hebrews 1:3 NIV, emphasis added

but comforting, father and mother all in one. The words weren't speaking love, they *were* love. Instantly, I recognized the Voice as that of the Lord's. I heard it just as clearly as if someone was standing over me speaking into my ear. It was real. To say it did not happen would be a lie. To disobey would be worse. What is interesting is, the message itself was stronger than the actual hearing, if that makes sense. I heard the Lord's voice say, "The Revelation of Jesus. Write the Revelation of Jesus." Immediately I knew in my spirit that it involved the Book of Revelation. I can't explain it other than I just knew that I knew. Strange. Why me? I'm no scholar. And like I said, the Book of Revelation was a bit blurry to me. Still, I innately knew that this assignment was inked on my heart as permanently as a tattoo.

A long time ago I gave Jesus my yes so there was not even a hint of saying no. It was an immediate "Yes, Lord," although I didn't know entirely what that yes would involve. I was simply struck by the invitation to write. And so, I began moving forward in faith with pen in hand, a teachable spirit, and a pliable heart. I was a notetaker for Jesus.

Then I saw it.

How could I not have seen it before?

It was right there the whole time, all those years. I'm sure I had seen it before but had skimmed right past it like we do with so many other lines and phrases in the Bible. The very first line in the Book of Revelation is "The Revelation of Jesus . . ." (Rev. 1:1 NKJV). The exact words the Voice had said. I thought I knew that but had always assumed it said ,"The Book of Revelation," but it doesn't. It opens up with

"The Revelation . . . of . . . Jesus . . ."

JESUS.

Now, He is something, or Someone rather, I could wrap my mind around—the exact representation of the invisible God.

As I said, I'm no scholar. I questioned, "Who am I to dive into all of this?" Then the Lord reminded me that I am His son, with the Holy Spirit residing inside me as teacher and guide. I can step out in faith and just follow His lead. I knew part of it would involve music, to write the Revelation of Jesus in song. How could it not with the Binions a part of it? Little did I know, however, that God would take that small step of faith and direct this project into so much more, involving TBN, a musical production, and this book. I merely became a vessel for the Holy Spirit to move through.

As a worshiper, my assignment was clear from the start. Write the Revelation of Jesus. Write what you see and hear, what the Holy Spirit illuminates. Lyrics. Melodies. About John and the pressure of Patmos, a cave of chaos and torture. Exiled. Boiled in oil. Left to die. Quarantined on a prison island. Then the encounter. The Unveiling. When I paused to really see, to take it all in, my imagination soared. I listened and could hear His voice like a rushing waterfall.

I was captured.

The songs practically wrote themselves.

Jesus was giving me a fresh revelation of Revelation. Not a new revelation, but an illumination of Scripture that had always been there. But I also understood that with this Revelation came a warning: "I warn everyone who hears the words of the prophecy of this scroll: If anyone adds anything to them, God will add to that person the plagues described in this scroll. And if anyone takes words away from this scroll of prophecy, God will take away from that person any share in the tree of life and in the Holy City, which are described in this scroll" (Rev. 22:18–19 NIV).

That is a serious admonition. So, with careful precision we tenderly walked the path of the last living apostle and, through the lens of worship, journaled his experience in word and song for a new generation of worshipers. We cautiously made sure that what we were writing in the music and the book were exactly what the Scriptures are saying and strove not to give an interpretation from any denominational viewpoint. He who has ears to hear, let him hear what the Spirit is saying. God is still speaking. He is inviting us to "come up higher" into the divine dance.

๑ ๑ ๑

The Book of Revelation is exactly what the opening sentence of the first chapter in the NKJV tells us: "The Revelation of Jesus Christ." Jesus is the messenger and the message. He was instructed by the Father and revealed that message to John. The word revelation is actually a translation of the Greek word *apokalupsis*, which means the removal of a veil so that something can be seen.[8] In the Book of Revelation, the great unveiling, the curtain of eternal things is pulled back, and we are invited to see the Apocalypse. The traditional dictionary is not altogether accurate when it defines Apocalypse as the final destruction of the world, or age. It is partly that, but it is significantly more. It should actually be defined as the unveiling of Jesus Christ's sovereign activity of judgment on the earth and the final ushering in of the Kingdom of God. In this revelation of things to come, we also see an unveiling of who Jesus truly is in the eternal realm. We see how much He loves His creation and to what lengths He went in order to restore all things, including us, back to Himself for eternity. "*. . . if I go and prepare a place for you,*

---

8   https://plato.stanford.edu/entries/divine-revelation; https://biblehub.com/
     greek/602.htm

I will come again and receive you to Myself; that where I am, there you may be also."[9] This is the end result of Revelation. Surprisingly, similar to the Book of Leviticus, the Book of Revelation is also a revelation of worship.

The apostle John encounters the Son of Man and is dazzled as heaven breaks into the cave where John is imprisoned on the Island of Patmos. Jesus, the glorious Lamb, unveils Himself, revealing His present, eternal majesty. John shows us the kinds of encounters that are possible between two worlds, between two dimensions. He proceeds to write down what he sees.

On one hand, John is elevated into the heavens and beholds in the Spirit realm things that are unfolding around the throne. Yet he is also fully aware of happenings in the physical realm on the earth. He weeps because no one in heaven or on earth is found worthy to open the seals on the scroll that's in the hand of the One seated on the throne. John is seeing this from both realities—heaven and earth. Then the angel proclaims, "Behold, the Lion of the tribe of Judah, the Root of David, has prevailed to open the scroll and to loose its seven seals" (Rev. 5:4–5 NKJV). John turns to see the Lion, but instead sees a Lamb. We begin to understand that things are not as they seem. This makes me wonder: Could John have seen from heaven's perspective the day when, on earth, Jesus stepped up in the synagogue, took the scroll of Isaiah, and broke the seal of understanding by declaring, in essence, that He was the One Isaiah was speaking of?[10] Then, as we will examine in detail later, there's the woman in John's vision who gives birth to a child (which is obviously Jesus) and a great dragon that tries to kill Him. This gives a whole new perspective of the Nativity.

I have discovered in my research that the Book of Revelation

---

9   John 14:3 NKJV
10   Luke 4:16–21

has over five hundred Old Testament references, causing one to consider that it is likely a concentrated version of the entirety of Biblical history. John beholds the One who was, and is, and is to come, and is quite possibly seeing history in the same way. Certainly, the Book of Revelation is filled with prophetic predictions of things to come, but it is impossible to ignore that John is retelling us the whole story of the Bible, capsulized into one final book. Revelation 1:3, the Scripture at the beginning of this chapter, says, "Blessed is the one who reads aloud the words of this prophecy." This means that Revelation is meant to be read out loud and be heard. That just resonates with me. The Revelation of Jesus is meant to be proclaimed out loud. It is meant to be heard. I feel like in many ways we've been duped by church denominations and organizations. We have been taught to be fearful of the Book of Revelation, when in fact it is an extraordinary, beautiful view of the glorious Jesus, and He's invited us to sit at the table with Him and partake. So, I invite you to come along with me on this journey in word and song. Go ahead: turn the page and enter into the divine dance and the Revelation of Jesus.

2

His head and his hairs were white like wool, as white as snow;
and his eyes were as a flame of fire; and his feet like unto fine brass,
as if they burned in a furnace; and his voice as the sound of many waters.

Revelation 1:14–15 KJV

Death obeyed Jesus' *command* when Jesus called Lazarus to come
forth after being in that dark and putrid tomb for four days. Nature
bowed to His *authority* when Jesus walked on the sea as if it were a
concrete sidewalk. The elements morphed to His *will* when Jesus
turned the water into wine and fed five thousand men (ten thousand
if you count the women and children) with only five loaves and two
fish. Blind eyes opening, storms calming, demons fleeing, withered
hands stretching out, lame walking . . . the list goes on and on.
And with awestruck wonder, John, along with the other disciples,
witnessed them all.

In addition to these miracles, John had stood nearby watching
as the finger of the Son of Man scribbled in the dirt, freeing with
His love the woman caught in her sin while her accusers were
shouting death. John was there when Mary Magdalene dumped a
pound of the most expensive perfume on Jesus' feet and then wiped
them with her hair. The room became saturated with the fragrance
of perfume and grace. Walking beside Jesus, John saw the broken
and bound set free, sinners forgiven and released to new life. He
had leaned in to hear the life-altering words that Messiah had to say
on any given subject. At the end of his Gospel, John wrote, "And

there are also many other things that Jesus did, which if they were
written one by one, I suppose that even the world itself could not
contain the books that would be written."[1] John had a way with
words and was obviously painting a picture for us of the magnitude
and magnificence of Jesus' works. William Barclay wrote of this
passage, "Human categories are powerless to describe Christ, and
human books are inadequate to hold him. And so John ends with
the innumerable triumphs, the inexhaustible power, and the limitless
grace of Jesus Christ."[2]

On one special occasion, sometime before Jesus' crucifixion,
John was invited with Peter and James to join Him on the top of
a mountain. When the four of them reached a certain point, Jesus
morphed right before their eyes. "There," wrote Matthew, "he
was transfigured before them. His face shone like the sun, and his
clothes became as white as the light."[3] As Jesus was standing in His
glorified state, Moses and Elijah appeared in their glorified state,
and the three of them started having a conversation. At that point, a
bright cloud surrounded everyone, and a voice boomed, "This is My
beloved Son, in whom I am well pleased. Hear Him!"[4] John, Peter,
and James were knocked flat on their faces and trembled with fear.
The encounter had such an impact on Peter that roughly thirty-five
years later, when he himself was about to be martyred as Jesus had
predicted, he said, "For we did not follow cunningly devised fables
when we made known to you the power and coming of our Lord
Jesus Christ but were eyewitnesses of His majesty. For He received
from God the Father honor and glory when such a voice came to
Him from the Excellent Glory: 'This is My beloved Son, in whom I

---

1   John 21:25 NKJV
2   Barclay, William. "Commentary on John 21:25". "William Barclay's Daily Study
     Bible". https://www.studylight.org/commentaries/dsb/john-21.html. 1956-1959.
3   Matthew 17:2 NIV
4   Matthew 17:5 NIV

am well pleased.' And we heard this voice which came from heaven when we were with Him on the holy mountain."[5]

Now, thirty or so years after Peter's death, all the other apostles have been martyred except John. He is an old man, and though the pastor-poet has not been killed, it isn't because his persecutors haven't tried. Historians tell us they attempted to kill John numerous times, but he simply would not die. Once, they tried to boil him alive in a cauldron of burning oil, but instead of screaming to death, he continued to preach. When they couldn't kill him, they determined to distance themselves from him by shipping him away to a cave on an escape-proof prison island. Why didn't boiling oil kill him? Surely his torturers left him in long enough for any human to die. Besides, they took joy in watching their victims suffer until death. History tells us it was a miracle on the scale of Shadrach, Meshach, and Abednego when they were thrown into the fiery furnace and did not burn. The esteemed and exhaustive second-century theologian/historian Tertullian wrote, "The apostle John, after being immersed in boiling oil and *taking no hurt*, is banished to an island."[6] Genelle Austin-Lett, professor at the College of Social Sciences and Director of Forensics Communication Studies at San Jose State University, said, "Histories of the Christian movement record that John was boiled in oil twice and didn't die. The second persecution of Christians under Domitian, A.D. 81 lists, 'Among the numerous martyrs that suffered during this persecution was Simeon, bishop of Jerusalem, who was crucified; and St. John, who was boiled in oil and afterward banished to Patmos.'"[7] *Foxe's Book of Martyrs* says, "Of John we are told, that when Domitian caused him to be apprehended as the very head and chief of the Christian

---

5   2 Peter 1:16–18 NKJV
6   *The Prescription of Heretics*, chapter XXXVI (emphasis added)
7   https://www.biblestudytools.com/history/foxs-book-of-martyrs/the-second-perse-cution-under-domitian-a-d-81.html

sect in all Asia, he also directed him to be brought to Rome. . . . On his arrival he was bound with cords, and cast into a cauldron of burning oil, to test the miraculous powers with which he claimed to be endowed, out of which fiery trial he came quite unhurt."[8] "Taking no hurt," "didn't die," and "quite unhurt"—sounds miraculous to me. Perhaps John was being supernaturally preserved for his final assignment, and to get it done, he had to be exiled. The highly respected Voice of the Martyrs affirms this:

> It is said that Roman emperor Domitian commanded that the apostle John be boiled to death in oil, but John only continued to preach from within the pot. Another time, John was forced to drink poison, but, as promised in Mark 16:18, it did not hurt him. Thus John, the head of the church in Ephesus at the time, was banished to Patmos in A.D. 97. John survived all of this because God had not finished with him yet. *A "revelation" still had to come.*[9]

Others, however, contend that John's body was indeed charred, along with all the horrors that come from being boiled in oil, yet he did not die. If this was the case, he would have been in intense physical pain and distress on the island, unable to move about, touch, or function without excruciating pain. Continuous treatment would have been necessary, or John would have likely died from infection. Not to mention, travel to the island by prisoner ship would have been agonizing. Most likely he would have been wrapped in cloth like a leper, requiring care. The distance from Rome to Patmos is over seven hundred nautical miles and would have taken eight to

---

8   John Foxe, *Foxe's Book of Martyrs* (Inspirational Promotions, Burlington, Ontario; 1960), 50.

9   https://www.persecutionblog.com/2006/09/boiled_in_oil_b.html (emphasis added)l

ten days. If you have ever visited the burn ward of a hospital, you've seen the pure agony burn patients are in. I can't imagine a severely burned individual making the trip, especially in the rough conditions of that day. Church history seems to support that John was boiled in oil, so I lean toward the former scenario of a miraculous intervention. The Bible does not mention that John was boiled in oil, but neither does it record Peter's upside-down crucifixion or Paul's beheading, yet both are established history. One thing is for certain: either way, God supernaturally preserved John's life for a divine assignment and continued to preserve him while on the island.

At the time of his banishment, John was pastor to seven churches in what is now Turkey. The churches were under intense persecution and were being snuffed out and scattered by the cruel Roman rule. Not only had the apostles been martyred because of the testimony of Jesus but also some of John's closest friends. John didn't know if he would ever see his churches again, so he began to pray . . . fervently. He prayed for days that turned to months. Prayer and communion with his God were his life on that island.

One day as he is praying, the atmosphere begins to shift. Suddenly John hears a loud voice behind him. He spins around to see who is speaking. As he turns, he sees a vision of seven golden lampstands, and among the lampstands stands someone like a Son of Man wearing a robe reaching down to his feet and a golden sash around his chest. And then, something that reminds him of his vision back on the Mount of Transfiguration: The heavenly man's hair is white like wool, as white as snow, and His eyes are like blazing fire. His voice sounds like a rushing waterfall. His face is like the brilliance of a million suns (Rev. 1:12–16).

It is of utmost importance to understand what John is describing. In the midst of the golden lampstands, he sees One like the Son of Man. The first time the term Son of Man is mentioned in the Bible is in the Book of Daniel. Along with that name, His heavenly physical nature is also described for the first time. The passage below from Daniel Chapter 7 is a bit long but critical. It is one of the main reasons the people of Israel had difficulty accepting Jesus as their Messiah.

> As I looked, thrones were set in place, and the Ancient of Days took his seat. His clothing was as white as snow; the hair of his head was white like wool. His throne was flaming with fire, and its wheels were all ablaze. A river of fire was flowing, coming out from before him. Thousands upon thousands attended him; ten thousand times ten thousand stood before him. The court was seated, and the books were opened. Then I continued to watch because of the boastful words the horn was speaking. I kept looking until the beast was slain and its body destroyed and thrown into the blazing fire. (The other beasts had been stripped of their authority, but were allowed to live for a period of time.) In my vision at night I looked, and there before me was one like a *son of man*, coming with the clouds of heaven. He approached the Ancient of Days and was led into his presence. He was given authority, glory and sovereign power; all nations and peoples of every language worshiped him. His dominion is an everlasting dominion that will not pass away, and his kingdom is one that will never be destroyed.[10]

Because of Daniel's vision of the Son of Man, Israel expected the Promised One to come in with great authority to overthrow Rome and free them from oppression. Jesus, however, came into the culture as a lowly, humble servant, the complete opposite of what

---

10   Daniel 7:9–14 NIV (emphasis added)

they were expecting. Yet Jesus still referred to Himself as the Son of Man. This blew their paradigm to bits! Throughout the four Gospels, Jesus declares to His followers that He is indeed the Son of Man. "Who do people say the Son of Man is?" He asked the disciples. Jesus knew exactly who He was, of course. He just wanted them to know. Most of us have heard the "Lord, liar, or lunatic" argument. If Jesus was not the Son of Man—God in the flesh—He was either a liar and deceiver on a scale the world has never known, or He was a complete lunatic. On top of that, it was unthinkable that the Messiah would hang out with sinners and outcasts, that He would have lunch with a prostitute or befriend dishonest tax collectors. What about washing the feet of His closest followers? Or, finally, being beaten, pierced, and nailed to a cross while those around hurled insults. "If You are the Christ, come down from the cross and save yourself!"[11] The Romans that Israel expected to be set free from were the ones executing Him. "How could this be our Messiah, the Son of Man?" they must have wondered.

They had seen the miracles, but it was the encounter on the Mount of Transfiguration that left no doubt who Jesus actually was, their only hope of salvation. Still, they couldn't understand the Son of Man suffering and dying on the cross. It didn't fit their paradigm either. The disciples wanted Jesus to call down legions of angels and destroy Rome and any other oppressors. But what they couldn't see was that something bigger than they could ever have imagined was going on. Jesus was defeating sin and bringing the entire universe into alignment. There was a spiritual war going on in the heavenly dimension. When Jesus took His last breath on the cross, He immediately went to work with eyes blazing, seizing the keys of death and Hades and the grave. He stripped the great beast of his power, overthrowing the entire kingdom of darkness

---

11   See Matthew 27:40

and making a show of him openly. Israel wanted Jesus to conquer Rome, but He had come to conquer sin and death, bringing the powers of darkness into legal submission! The Son of Man from Daniel's vision was now demonstrating His ultimate rule.

In the interim, between the death of Jesus on the cross and John's exile on the Island of Patmos, the church was born and began to thrive. Thousands were coming into this new kingdom. The fire of God had begun to burn in the hearts of every believer, but not without resistance and persecution. Rome still governed and was determined to crush the church. And now John has been arrested, tortured, and left to die on a prison island. But his life spent with Jesus, seeing Him in His full glory on the Mount of Transfiguration and then resurrected from the grave, plus empowerment from the indwelling Holy Spirit that Jesus had promised, has kept John strong through all the persecution and pain. And so, he prays. He prays past the isolation and loneliness of the cave, past the physical suffering, until he enters the Spirit realm. He hears trumpet blasts and rushing water and turns to see. There He is! Unapproachable light, extending an invitation to draw near. It's the Son of Man just as he had seen Him on the mountain.

John is instructed to write what he hears and sees. And in so doing, he allows us to see. With our imaginations soaring, we step into the realm of the fantastical. It is the Great Unveiling, the Revelation of Jesus. "The revelation from Jesus Christ, which God gave him to show his servants what must soon take place. He made it known by sending his angel to his servant John, who testifies to everything he saw—that is, the word of God and the testimony of Jesus Christ. Blessed is the one who reads aloud the words of this prophecy and blessed are those who hear it and take to heart what is written in it, because the time is near" (Rev. 1:1–3 NIV).

THE REVELATION OF JESUS

Mitch Wong, David Binion, Steffany Gretzinger, Krissy Nordhoff,
Gracie Binion

Verse 1

This is the revelation
Of Jesus Christ
This is the great unveiling
The end of time
Heavenly poetry
Reveals the mystery
This is the Revelation

Chorus

Blessings come to the one who reads (the revelation, the revelation)
Blessings come to the one who proclaims
(the revelation, the revelation)
Blessings come to the one who listens
(the revelation, the revelation)
Blessings come to the one who obeys
(the revelation, the revelation)

Verse 2

He is the Faithful Witness
The First to rise
From death's cold womb is given
Eternal life
More than a prophecy
He is reality
This is the Revelation

BRIDGE
Give us eyes to see
Give us ears to hear
Come and fill our hearts
With a holy fear
Coming with the clouds
You are drawing near
We are waiting now
We are waiting here

3

PATMOS

I, John, your brother and companion in the suffering and kingdom and patient endurance that are ours in Jesus, was on the island of Patmos because of the word of God and the testimony of Jesus.

Revelation 1:9 NIV

Patmos, a small Greek island, was once inhabited for approximately three thousand years. However, it fell when Rome seized control of territories in that region. The inhabitants fled and the island became deserted. The Romans decided to use it to imprison criminals. It was known as a prison island, much as Alcatraz is known today. Surrounded by the Aegean Sea, jagged rocks, and mountain cliffs, it was impossible to escape. Prisoners were sentenced to a life of survival against the harsh and unforgiving elements. Banishment in that time was considered one of the worst forms of punishment, not only because of the rugged environment but because the isolation and separation from everyone you knew and loved was emotionally unbearable. One thing is for certain: Patmos was no resort, and because of his testimony for Jesus, this was John's new home.

Yet if John had learned anything during his time with Jesus, it was how to pray. He had watched as Jesus withdrew from the crowds to be alone and commune with His Father. He had soaked up Jesus' words when He instructed the disciples how to pray. John was one of the three invited by Jesus to the Garden of Gethsemane, where Jesus prayed in agony and was then captured. It was John who wrote about Jesus seeing Nathanael under the fig tree. Consider the story as it applies to John now on Patmos. The story is recorded in John Chapter 1. "Jesus saw Nathanael coming toward Him, and said of him, 'Behold, an Israelite indeed, in whom is no deceit!' Nathanael asked, 'How do You know me?' Jesus answered, 'Before Philip called you, when you were under the fig tree, I saw you.' Nathanael responded, 'Rabbi, You are the Son of God! You are the King of Israel!'"[1] The reason Nathanael got so excited was that he knew Jesus hadn't physically been there to see him under that tree, not in the natural realm. Most scholars believe Nathanael had been praying in a private location, as was the custom of Jews in that day. Some contend he was in deep intercession, longing for the coming Messiah. At any rate, that particular fig tree was an important spot for him, a sacred place of communion. It was likely he had encountered God there. Charles Spurgeon wrote:

> He [Nathanael] had looked around the garden and fastened the gate so that no one might come in, and he had poured into the ear of his God some very tender confession, under the shade of the fig tree. When Christ said to him, "When you were under the fig tree," it brought to his memory how he poured out his broken and his contrite spirit, and confessed sins unknown to all except God.… Or under the fig tree he had been engaged in very earnest prayer. Was that fig tree to Nathanael what Peniel was to Jacob, a place where he had wrestled until the break of day, pleading with God? Once more, it may be that under that fig tree he had enjoyed the sweetest communion with his God.[2]

---

1   John 1:43–51 NKJV

2   Charles Spurgeon, "921. Nathanael and the Fig Tree" (a sermon delivered March 20, 1870, at Metropolitan Tabernacle, Newington, UK), Answers in Genesis, December 16, 2011, https://answersingenesis.org/ education/Spurgeon-sermons/921-nathanael-and-the-figtree/.

In a way, the cave on Patmos was John's fig tree. He knew that Jesus saw him.

Some fifty days after the resurrection, John discovered fully the power of a bended knee. He had gathered in an upper room with the others at the instruction of the resurrected Jesus. And they waited. They waited and they prayed. Until a rushing wind. A fiery invasion. Heaven invaded the room, and they were filled with the Holy Spirit. The infant church began to breathe the life of heaven, and the world was turned upside down. The 120 in the Upper Room quickly turned into 3,120. And so, the story of the church began. Speaking of the apostles and the new believers, Luke wrote in Acts, "These who have turned the world upside down have come here."[3]

But now on Patmos it seems that all is lost. However, "The LORD is close to the brokenhearted and saves those who are crushed in spirit," wrote the Psalmist,[4] and He was certainly close to John. Holed away in a cave, John would not have been blamed if he had chosen to surrender to his plight and just give up. But giving up was never an option. Nor does John sensationalize his condition. If it weren't for the writings of other historians, we wouldn't know the details of his torture, because he doesn't tell us. His only description is, "I, John, your companion in suffering…was on the island of Patmos because of the word of God and the testimony of Jesus" (Rev. 1:9 NIV). Despite his suffering and circumstances that screamed defeat, John knew Jesus was real, alive, and fully present. The Holy Spirit inside him had become his ever-present Comforter.

His seven churches are struggling. He's struggling, yet John has seen and experienced too much to give up. Alone in that dark cave, he begins to cry out to God and reach toward the heavens. John

---

3   Acts 17:6 NKJV
4   Psalm 34:18 NIV

knows, though, that he can never touch the hem of Jesus' heavenly garment until his knees touch the ground. So, he positions himself physically and postures his heart and begins to press. He prays until he loses all sense of knowing what to say with his mouth or grasp with his thoughts. Days pass as he continually pursues and presses in. Then the Lord's Day comes, the day his seven congregations normally gather. John feels that his prayers are finding traction. Something stirs in his heart and the dark cave starts to glow as the familiar sense of God's presence begins to swirl around him. Beauty breaks though the brokenness. The cave of darkness is transformed into light. The pressure of Patmos can't compare to the weight of God's glory.

John demonstrates to us what is possible for the one who will pray. The message isn't to tell us how bad our world is but to encourage us not to succumb to the pressure of tribulation. Every generation has experienced its own set of struggles and trials. Every nation has known political upheaval. The church has been able to navigate its way through severe oppression in every situation. Perhaps you find yourself in your own personal Patmos, unable to see your way out of the dark cave of separation. Let John's story inspire you. There are encounters awaiting that God wants to have with His people. He wants us to know that there is beauty on the Island of Patmos.

PATMOS
Mitch Wong and David Binion

Verse 1
Beaten, abused

Boiled, and bruised

Somehow, I keep on breathing

Slave to the truth

Exiled, accused

The wages of my believing

But I don't have to be afraid

I know who's with me in this cave

Chorus
Even in my darkest hour

I know there's a fresh encounter

Find me on my knees

My heart still believes

I can recognize Your presence

Drawing me to highest heaven

Find me on my knees

Let my spirit see

There's beauty on the island of Patmos

4

IN THE SPIRIT ON THE LORD'S DAY

On the Lord's Day I was in the Spirit,
and I heard behind me a loud voice like a trumpet.

Revelation 1:10 NIV

"On the Lord's Day I was in the Spirit. . ." I don't think it was
an accident that John gives us this significant detail. The Passion
paraphrase says it like this: "I was in the Spirit *realm* on the Lord's
Day" (Rev. 1:10 TPT, emphasis added). The natural tendency of
the flesh when we are going through trials or tough situations is to
pull away from God and attempt to cope with things on our own,
in our own strength. Some even get angry at God for allowing their
trials to come. Others think they've done something wrong or doubt
their faith. Never mind that Jesus Himself said, "In this world you
will have trouble. But take heart! I have overcome the world."[1] Some
of God's choice servants with the most faith experienced deep trials
and tribulation. Just read the second half of Hebrews Chapter 11,
the great Hall of Faith. Despite his grueling circumstances, John
made a deliberate choice to keep his eyes focused and his heart
postured toward God. A model for us all, he didn't blame God or
pull away in his difficult circumstance. Instead, he pressed in closer
through worship and prayer.

It's quite possible to be in a prison of circumstance and be
in the Spirit at the same time. At the time John was suffering on

---

1   John 16:33 NIV

Patmos, isolated in that cave, he was also in the Spirit. Think about that. That means God was fully present in the midst of his pain and difficulties, and He is fully present in ours. Surely John felt the silence of God for days and possibly months before his breakthrough. Often the silence of God is loud, but we can press in and break through the silence. A more literal translation of Revelation 1:10 is ". . . I came to be in the Spirit."[2] John was no longer simply thinking *about* God or even talking *to* God, he was being drawn into more of Him, becoming one with Him. A merging was taking place that continued until a bursting forth of the Spirit. John "came to be in the Spirit." Only when we concentrate and fully focus will we engage in the power of prayer. Prayer is more than petitioning God for things and for deliverance from difficult situations. It is drawing near to Him and coming into His awareness. "If we draw near to God," James wrote, "He will draw near to us."[3] What an incredible promise.

Like a loving parent sitting on a sofa who scoots closer to embrace their child who has crawled up to be close to them, God responds to our crawling up to Him by shifting closer to us and embracing us. As much as we want an encounter with God, He wants an encounter with us.

Paul wrote to the church in Ephesians, "And God raised us up with Christ and seated us with Him in heavenly places."[4] This was not a message to the church solely to tell us where we go when we die. It was also a positional reality in the Spirit *realm* that is available to us now. Paul sent this letter to the church at Ephesus, one of the seven churches that the apostle John oversaw.

When John prayed with great fervor, he unlocked a door and

---

2   https://www.quotescosmos.com/bible/bible-verses/Revelation-1-10.html
3   James 4:8 (my paraphrase)
4   Ephesians 2:6 NIV

found himself in another realm on visible display. The dullness of his surroundings dissipated, and the spectacular realities of another dimension became fully alive before him. Paul also stated in Romans, "You, however, are not in the realm of the flesh but are in the realm of the Spirit, if indeed the Spirit of God lives in you. And if anyone does not have the Spirit of Christ, they do not belong to Christ."[5]

Of course, God is sovereign and that is something we must understand. He knows all things and is working all things together for His purposes. He had John chosen from the beginning to write the Revelation of Jesus. He knew John would be in that cave on Patmos drawing near. God knew John would be in a position to receive. We work together with God in partnership. The Bible clearly teaches that God is in control, that He predestined us, and that He knows beforehand what we are going to do. The Bible also clearly teaches that we have free will and must choose by faith to believe and act in obedience. It is a mystery that we will understand fully in eternity. For now, according to Hebrews, "He is a rewarder of those who diligently seek Him."[6] The implication is clear. If we don't diligently seek Him, we don't get the reward. But what is the reward? It's many things, but first and foremost, the reward is Himself, His manifest presence. Regarding this passage, nineteenth-century Scottish theologian Alexander MacLaren said, "The best reward of seeking is to find the thing that you are looking for. So, the best reward that God, the Rewarder, gives is when He gives Himself."[7]

John did not receive what he wrote in Revelation by sitting around on a Sunday with nothing to do, waiting for something

---

5   Romans 8:9 NIV, emphasis added
6   Hebrews 11:6 NKJV
7   Expositions of Holy Scripture, Alexander MacLaren, https://biblehub.com/commentaries/maclaren/hebrews/11.htm

interesting to happen. He was praying. Drawing near. Diligently seeking God. He was putting himself in a posture to receive. He "came to be in the Spirit." John already had the Holy Spirit inside him, but "in the Spirit" is a greater manifestation. Robert Jamieson, A. R. Fausset, and David Brown wrote in their 1882 commentary on this verse:

> In the Spirit—in a state of ecstasy; the outer world being shut out, and the inner and higher life or spirit being taken full possession of by God's Spirit, so that an immediate connection with the invisible world is established. While the prophet "speaks" in the Spirit, the apocalyptic seer is in the Spirit in his whole person. The spirit only (that which connects us with God and the invisible world) is active, or rather recipient, in the apocalyptic state. With Christ this being "in the Spirit" was not the exception, but His continual state.[8]

John was experiencing this manifestation of the Spirit smack-dab in the middle of his suffering, great pain, and great joy. Prayer like this combines the experiences of being on Patmos and being in the Spirit. This kind of revelation comes only to the person who prays. Sometimes God does His greatest works when we are in prison. John's story on Patmos reminds me of John Bunyan, the author of the classic allegory *The Pilgrim's Progress*. With over 250 million copies sold, it is the most read book outside of the Bible.[9] Millions have been drawn closer to Jesus and received comfort and salvation because of this book. In 1661, Bunyan was thrown into prison for preaching the gospel and holding church services.

---

8   *A Commentary, Critical, Practical, and Explanatory on the Old and New Testaments* by Robert Jamieson, A. R. Fausset and David Brown [1882]
9   https://www.thetrails.org/blog/post/pilgrims-progress-

He remained imprisoned for twelve years. Think of it...twelve years. Bunyan was a prayer warrior and spent the time in his cell reading and praying, drawing near to God. God became his closest companion in that prison. He had two books during that time: the Holy Bible and a copy of *Foxe's Book of Martyrs*. Then one night he had a supernatural breakthrough into the Spirit realm in the form of a divine dream that set the idea of *The Pilgrim's Progress* into motion. From there his prison cell became the place where he could write undistracted. He penned the epic *Pilgrim's Progress* along with a couple other books. John Bunyan said, "Prayer is a sincere, sensible, affectionate pouring out of the soul to God." Undoubtedly, this is what John was doing in the cave on the Lord's Day and had been doing every day.

When you arrive at this place called "in the Spirit," you are more conscious of spiritual things than you are of natural things. Jesus gave us a glimpse when He transfigured before Peter, James, and John, reflecting images of a greater reality. He hinted at this reality when He announced that His kingdom was at hand. He told them to repent, which means to change the way you think so that you may grasp what is right in front of you. In essence, Jesus was declaring to them that His kingdom was within their reach. He declared. On Patmos, John understood this and had to pray himself beyond his limitations and the distraction of his physical pain.

It's interesting that he found himself in the Spirit "on the Lord's Day" and not on the Sabbath day. The Sabbath was never referred to as the Lord's Day. Had John meant that, he would have said he was in the Spirit on the Sabbath day. Theologians differ as to where this term "the Lord's Day" originated, but the general consensus is that Jesus was resurrected on the first day of the week, which we know is a Sunday. Almost all commentaries agree. *The Pulpit Commentary* says, "There can be little doubt but that 'the first day of the week,' the Christian Sunday, is meant."[10] Jesus was arrested on a Thursday, crucified on a Friday morning, and placed in the tomb early that evening. There was no activity on that following Saturday, as all Jewish people were observing the Sabbath. Not until the first day of the week, Sunday, do we see things begin to move. The women went to the tomb to anoint His body and found the stone rolled away. Instead of finding the body of Jesus, they discovered an empty tomb and an angel who announced, "He has risen!"[11] Because He was resurrected on a Sunday, the first day of the week, that day would eventually become known as the Lord's Day. Every Sunday following would then be recognized as the same, but that first Easter morning is where it began. Some even suggest that John could have had his encounter on an Easter Sunday. If this is indeed the case, the deeper layers of understanding reveal an even greater declaration, as John announced that he was in the Spirit realm, on the anniversary of our resurrected Lord, the Lord's Day." This is the day that John's seven congregations gathered together to worship and pray. John does not know how they are managing life in these churches, and he of course is concerned. And it's on behalf of these seven churches that Jesus reveals Himself, giving specific instruction to each one.

So, the praying pastor, the intense and passionate intercessor, presses into the Spirit realm and is given vision and understanding that transform the tortured exile into a most energetic prophet. Visions, if they are truly visions, make things happen. John the

---

10   *The Pulpit Commentary*, Electronic Database. Copyright © 2001, 2003, 2005, 2006, 2010 by Biblesoft, Inc.

11   Matthew 28:1–15; Luke 24:1–12; John 20:1–10

exiled is now John the empowered because of the vision. From Patmos he ascends into the realm of the Spirit and is given a vision of Christ. He returns to the cave as a pastor with power. Rome tried to shut him up, no longer to be seen or heard, but the Spirit lifted him up and filled his eyes with visions and his mouth with encouraging words that have given direction to churches ever since.

I WAS IN THE SPIRIT ON THE LORD'S DAY

David Binion and Krissy Nordhoff

VERSE 1

I was in the Spirit on the Lord's Day
Caught up in the fire as Your eyes blazed
I see You

Draped across Your chest a sash of glory
Your head, Your hair, the purest white, are glowing
I see You
I see You

So beautiful
The One who was, and is, the One who's coming
So powerful
The One who is the End and the Beginning

CHORUS

Behold, He's coming on the clouds
Behold, He's coming here and now
And the only word, the only word that I can speak is "holy"

VERSE 2

I can hear the sound of heaven falling
Your voice an endless waterfall, it's roaring
I hear You
I hear You

BRIDGE
May all honor, and all glory
Be Yours forever, Yours forever
May the power, and dominion
Be Yours forever, Yours forever

5

I SEE JESUS

Then I turned to see the voice that spoke with me.
And having turned I saw seven golden lampstands,
and in the midst of the seven lampstands One like the Son of Man....

Revelation 1:12-13 NKJV

"Have you seen Him? Have you seen Him? Have you seen my lover?" It was the urgent cry of despair from the sleepy-eyed Shulamite bride in the Song of Solomon. She had waited too long to respond to the knock at the door. "It was Him! I know it was Him! I could smell His fragrance when I finally opened the door." But His fragrance was the only thing that remained. She ran through the streets desperately searching, asking anyone who would listen, "Have you seen Him? Have you seen my lover?" Finally, she cries out to the women in the city, "I charge you, O daughters of Jerusalem, if you find my beloved, that you tell him I am lovesick!"[1] It is a sobering scenario that we must consider. How many moments of intimacy have we missed?

Then there was Moses, who caught a glimpse of Him in a fiery bush, uncertain of what he was beholding until he heard the voice. "Take off your shoes, you're standing on holy ground."[2] Not exactly a face-to-face encounter, but a supernatural encounter indeed. Moses could see Him in the sound of His voice. There was

---

1   Song of Solomon 5:2–8 NKJV
2   Exodus 3:5

just something about God's voice that convinced Moses to obey. Many years later, Moses found himself on the mountain crying out, "Please, show me Your glory!"[3]

"No one can see my face and live"[4] came the response. But the desperation in Moses' cry touched the heart of God in such a way that moved Him to reveal Himself, but only from His backside as He passed by. Moses saw Him from behind.[5] The encounter affected Moses so dramatically that his face glowed when he returned to the people of Israel.

Nebuchadnezzar saw Him in the furnace with the three Hebrew men as one who looks like the Son of God.[6]

Isaiah saw Him high and lifted up, and the train of His robe filled the temple.[7]

Ezekiel saw Him as a wheel in the middle of a wheel.[8]

Daniel saw the magnificent, glorious image of the One whose robe was white as snow, with hair white like wool and a throne of fire.[9]

Other prophets saw Him and declared that He would come.

Mary gave birth to the Messiah and beheld the little baby face of God. She watched Him grow and mature. She watched Him turn water to wine and heal the sick. Then she watched Him be tortured and crucified.

John the Baptist saw Him and declared, "Behold! The Lamb of God who takes away the sin of the world!"[10]

---

3   Exodus 33:18 TLV
4   Exodus 33:20
5   Exodus 33:20-23
6   Daniel 3:25
7   Isaiah 6:1
8   Ezekiel 1:1–21
9   Daniel 7:9
10   John 1:29 NKJV

Peter the apostle declared on behalf of all the disciples, "We . . . . . . were eyewitnesses of His majesty!"[11]

John, along with Peter and James, had experienced the transfiguration on the mountain and seen the glorious image of Jesus that Daniel described back in the seventh chapter of Daniel. Now, many years later, John is in a cave on an island seeing Jesus in His radiant glory once again. "I SEE JESUS! His hair! His eyes! His feet! His hands! The brightness! Oh, what brilliance! How magnificent!"

I must ask, have you seen Him? Perhaps in a dream? Or in a vision? Men still dream dreams and see visions. If not, that's okay. It doesn't mean you are not spiritual. You have the Scriptures, His Word, which, according to Peter, is a surer word.[12] Oh yes, you have seen Him. Maybe in stories you've heard in Sunday school. You could see His hands break the loaves and feed the five thousand. What about the sermons describing the crucifixion? I know I have. I could see His bloodied body suspended in the air on wooden beams. I could hear His cry, "Father, forgive them!"[13] I could imagine the whole scenario. I could see Him. And I also imagined that He could see me. And I was undone. I realized that unless I could allow myself to see His passion for me, my worship could never be authentic. Worship in its best definition is "love responding to love." To see Him, to behold His love, unlocks the resources of affection in our hearts and we explode with worship. No one has to teach us what to say or what to do. I see Jesus! Oh yes, I see Jesus!

When John begins this final book of the Bible with the words "the Revelation of Jesus Christ," we understand first that the Revelation is about Jesus. And secondly, the Revelation comes from

---

11   2 Peter 1:16 NKJV
12   2 Peter 1:19–21
13   Luke 23:34

Jesus. He is showing His servants things that will come to pass, along with warnings, exhortations, and glimpses of heaven and the spiritual realm. But first and foremost, Jesus is revealing Himself as fully God. He wants there to be no misunderstanding about that. The Book of Revelation is a proclamation by Jesus about Himself. It is *not* simply information on how bad the world we live in is, nor is it a report on the persecution of the church.

After a few introductory sentences, John tells us about the loud voice reverberating like a trumpet behind him saying, "I am the Alpha and the Omega, the First and the Last,"[14] and, "What you see, write in a book and send it to the seven churches which are in Asia: to Ephesus, to Smyrna, to Pergamos, to Thyatira, to Sardis, to Philadelphia, and to Laodicea" (Rev. 1:11 NKJV). John then turns to see the voice, and what he witnesses takes his breath away. "And having turned I saw seven golden lampstands, and in the midst of the seven lampstands One like the Son of Man, clothed with a garment down to the feet and girded about the chest with a golden band. His head and hair were white like wool, as white as snow, and His eyes like a flame of fire; His feet were like fine brass, as if refined in a furnace, and His voice as the sound of many waters; He had in His right hand seven stars, out of His mouth went a sharp two-edged sword, and His countenance was like the sun shining in its strength"(vv. 1:12–16 NKJV).

It is necessary for us to understand that Jesus is revealing Himself in the midst of the churches. His desire is to be discovered in His church, to be seen by the company of believers, the Body of Christ. When John witnesses Jesus standing in the midst of the lampstands, he describes Him as One like the Son of Man. As we have seen, the Son of Man is a glorious image that commands our

---

14   This is one place Jesus reveals Himself as God.

attention. Darrel Johnson gives great insight on this in his book *Discipleship on the Edge*. I gleaned much of the following information from his writings. The description of Jesus in His glorified state begins with His clothing—a long robe with a golden belt-like girdle wrapped around His chest. (One translation calls it a sash.) This royal garment defines His role. He is dressed in what was prescribed for Aaron in his priestly work.[15] The earthly tabernacle and priestly garments were ordered to be constructed as likenesses of the eternal realities in heaven. The Son of Man is not only God, but He is also a priest, our High Priest after the order of Melchizedek. The sash draped across His chest means the work is finished. The sash would be around His waist if He was still at work. His clothing in heaven reflects that, and it should determine how we interact with Him from earth. When we see a person in a police officer's uniform, we are given an understanding of who that person will be when we draw close to them and interact. Their uniform reflects their position and the way we respond. Likewise, this priestly dress of the Son of Man shapes how we are called to respond and interpret what we see during John's vision. A priest is a mediator between us and God. In Hebrew, He is a *dalet*, which means doorway.[16]

Jesus, the Son of Man, is our high priest, our doorway. He lives to intercede for us. Though He is God, He was a man with passions and struggles just like us. He understands our frailties and that we are but dust. As believers we have Him inside us, with all His power and authority and comfort and grace available to us through His Holy Spirit. If we find ourselves in a personal storm and regret the mess we have made, Jesus our High Priest promises help. If we struggle with devastating news from the doctor, our high priest offers hope. Because the Son of Man reveals Himself as our priest, there

---

15   Exodus 29:5
16   https://hebrewtoday.com/alphabet/the-letter-dalet-%D7%93/

is nothing to be afraid of. In our churches, a priest or pastor is an approachable figure, someone we can relate to. Jesus came to us and became a man so that we could come to Him unafraid. While His image is magnificent and fearsome and terrifying, His attire invites us to come to Him as a son or daughter. He knows — our sin. He knows our baggage, our despair and struggle. Let Him embrace and comfort you. Let Him walk with you and stand with you. You are His. He died for you and rose again to be your great and perfect High Priest.

After the clothing, the first things we look at in a person are their head and eyes, which are a window into their core. The head and eyes of the Son of Man reveal Him as compassionate and forgiving, yet commanding and fierce. This priest is the One who gives evidence that all is pure between us and God. He is pure. "His head and His hair were white as wool, white as snow" (Rev. 1:14 NKJV).

Remember the prophet's promise: "Though your sins are like scarlet, they shall be as white as snow . . . they shall be as wool."[17] And the psalmist's prayer: "Purge me with hyssop, and I shall be clean; wash me, and I shall be whiter than snow."[18] That's what happens when we trust and believe in Jesus' provision on the cross and His imputed righteousness. "God made him who had no sin to be sin for us, so that in him we might become the righteousness of God."[19] He made a way where there was no way. Christ is the fulfilled promise and the answered prayer—clean, holy. His head and hair were the brightest white, representing His purity.

His eyes were "like a flame of fire" (Rev. 1:14 NKJV). We mentioned examples in the beginning of this chapter of the

---

17   Isaiah 1:18 NKJV
18   Psalm 51:7 NKJV
19   2 Corinthians 5:21 NIV

various images of the fiery display as we look into the eyes of
the Son of Man: the burning bush that Moses encountered and
Nebuchadnezzar's fiery furnace, and let's not forget the fiery
chariots that separated Elijah and Elisha. Fire penetrates and brings
transformation. It purifies. Holiness gets inside us and changes us.
The eyes of Jesus penetrate and purify us. He is a consuming fire.
His nature is so completely pure that as He looks into our eyes and
our hearts, His gaze destroys all that is not pure. He is perfect and
holy. He is awesome and loving. His love and holiness obliterate sin
in our lives and ultimately in the universe. He *will* have purity. God
is holy, He is flawless, He is pure. I'm not saying that the fire will
burn us if we do not worship, but I am saying that His fire will burn
in us until we can't resist worship, and it will go on burning until all
that is foreign surrenders to its force, the presence of God.

"His feet were like fine brass, as if refined in a furnace" (Rev.
1:15 NKJV). This brilliant image tells us of Christ's kingdom set on
a solid foundation. The bronze base is firm. Bronze is a combination
of iron and copper. Iron is strong but rusts. Copper won't rust but
is pliable. Combine the two into bronze and the best qualities of
each are preserved: the strength of the iron and the endurance of
the copper. The rule of Christ is built on this base. The foundation
of His power has been tested by fire. When John describes Jesus as
having feet of bronze, we see Him standing strong.

In the first chapter of his Gospel, John writes, "In the beginning
was the Word, and the Word was with God, and the Word was God.
He was with God in the beginning. Through him all things were
made; without him nothing was made that has been made."[20]Jesus
is the Word, and John shows us a Christ *speaking*. The Bible begins
with God speaking, speaking into existence first creation and then

---

20   John1:1-3 NIV

redemption. The word God speaks is important. How something is said often matters as much as what is said. Tone conveys a lot. We interpret words by means of sound. The meaning of a word is conveyed by the nuances of the voice, which prepares us to understand with our minds. So, before we are told what the Son of Man says, we are introduced to His way of speaking: ". . . and His voice as the sound of many waters" (Rev. 1:16 NKJV). It describes the sound of His voice. His voice is as stunning as His appearance, magnificent in every way!

Our response, even before we comprehend His message, is being shaped into extravagant worship. John introduces us to this incredible image of Jesus holding seven stars in His right hand. The right hand speaks of authority, control, and omnipotence. Jesus holds the stars in His right hand. He runs the cosmos. It is that simple. He controls the planets. And if He controls the planets, He is capable of seeing us through our darkest tribulation.

There are seven images described in John's vision:

- The *first* and *seventh* images were His white head and shining face. They tell us of forgiveness and blessing.

- The *second* and *sixth* images were His eyes and mouth and speak to us of relationship. Sight and sound are the way we communicate. Jesus is revealing that God is in relationship with us.

- The *third* and *fifth* images were His feet and right hand. Feet represent stability and action, the right hand, authority, control, and omnipotence.

- The *fourth* image of the *seven* is the voice. It is at the center. All prophetic and apostolic words converge in this voice that thunders like a roaring waterfall.

John's vision is both *heard* and *seen*. We see Jesus' head, hair, eyes, feet, hand, and face, and we hear His thundering voice. Throughout Scripture all of these are the source of revelation. These magnificent images of Jesus express so many characteristics and attributes of the almighty Lord who is and was and is to come.

ৡ৹   ৡ৹   ৡ৹

The vision John sees in this first chapter is the most elaborate vision of Christ in the Book of Revelation but not the only one. There is also a vision of the Lamb standing "as though it had been slain" (Rev. 5:6–7), showing the action of redemption. Then there's the vision of the birth of Jesus (Rev. 12:1–6); the vision of the Lamb surrounded by the 144,000 (Rev. 14:1); the Son of Man crowned and armed for judgment (Rev. 14:14); and the vision of Christ mounted and leading the armies of heaven, "King of kings and Lord of lords" (Rev. 19:16). Finally, there is the Christ of the second coming (Rev. 22:12–17). In all seven of these visions John sees Jesus and is instructed to write what he sees.

As we conclude this chapter, I must ask again: Can you see Him? John wrote down what he saw in hopes that we would be able to see for ourselves. Revelation is not so much about what is to come as it is about what is now. Yes, we will see Him on that final day when we enter into the eternal realm. But if you will align your vision with your heart's desire to behold, maybe you can say with certainty, "I see Jesus!"

I SEE JESUS
Mitch Wong and David Binion

Verse 1
Voice like rushing waters
Hair like purest snow
Eyes like flames of fire
Feet like bronze aglow
From His face comes blinding light
From His mouth a two-edged blade
The terrifying beauty
The wonder has a Name

Chorus
Jesus
Jesus
Jesus
I see Jesus

Verse 2
Alpha and Omega
The First One and The Last
Beginning and Completion
The Lion and the Lamb
The Root and Branch of David
The Bright and Morning Star
The Word of God, The Amen
But the Name above them all . . .

CHORUS
Jesus
Jesus
Jesus
I see Jesus

6

As for the mystery of the seven stars that you saw in my right hand,
and the seven golden lampstands, the seven stars are the angels
of the seven churches, and the seven lampstands are the seven churches.

Revelation 1:20 ESV

Sin divides, separates, and sentences us to solitary
confinement. The gospel of "Good News," on the other hand,
forgives, cleanses, and restores us to a right relationship with
our Creator. The Holy Spirit comes inside us, and because He
is our constant companion, we need never be alone, even if we
are banished to a cave on a forsaken island. Yet even though
circumstances sometimes force us to be alone, or stand alone, the
Christian life is meant to be lived out in a community of believers.
Through the gospel we are not only reconciled to God, but we
are adopted into His family, His household, the Body of Christ,
the church. "Now, therefore, you are no longer strangers and
foreigners, but fellow citizens with the saints and members of the
household of God."[1]

In the Old Testament, understanding of "the house" was
primarily limited to material structures and the house of the Lord
as the physical temple. Israel's history was rich with grand images of
the tabernacle of Moses, David's tabernacle, and finally Solomon's
grand temple. Building the permanent temple was David's

---

1   Ephesians 2:19 NKJV

passionate desire, but because of his blood-stained hands, God did not allow it. The baton, however, was passed to his son Solomon, who fulfilled David's dream. "I was glad when they said to me, 'Let us go into the house of the LORD,'" David penned.[2] The Holy Spirit, moving prophetically through David and speaking of the coming Messiah, wrote, "For zeal for your house consumes me."[3] The disciples were reminded of this psalm when Jesus passionately flipped the tables in the temple, scattering coins and doves and parchments, then cracked a whip with divine authority and drove out the money changers.[4] Both the Old Testament saints and the disciples that walked with Jesus had an understanding of "the house" that was limited to physical structures and the Spirit of God dwelling in the temple.

Jacob was the first person in all of Scripture to use the term "house of God."[5] Interestingly, it had nothing to do with a physical structure or temple. Sleeping out under the stars with a rock as a pillow, he awoke from a dream about angels ascending and descending on a ladder extending from heaven to earth. His words were "Surely the LORD is in this place . . . . How awesome is this place! . . . Surely the Lord is in this place. . . This is none other than the house of God; this is the gate of heaven."[6] In the wilderness, there was no physical structure, there were no stained-glass windows or walls or doors. Jacob named the place Bethel, which means "House of God." But the truth is, Jacob could have had this encounter in any geographical location. It had nothing to do with location but everything to do with the person. Jacob's encounter would serve as a prophetic picture of God's new covenant House,

---

2   Psalm 122:1 NKJV
3   Psalm 69:9 NIV
4   John 2:17
5   Genesis 28:16–17 NIV
6   ibid.

made with living stones. When the Church was born in the Book of Acts, new insight was given as thousands were filled with the Holy Spirit and began to function as the temple of God. Instantly, His temple moved from brick-and-mortar walls into walls made of flesh. "Do you not know," Paul urged, "that your bodies are temples of the Holy Spirit, who is in you? . . ."[7] We still meet in physical buildings dedicated as places of gathering, but we've come to understand that the gate of heaven is wherever we happen to be.

In the Book of Revelation, once we grasp the awesome encounter John is having, we see right away that the message isn't *to* John but *through* John *for* the seven churches, the living stones that make up the House of God. This family of believers, living stones, is also compared to a physical body with individual parts, each with their unique function, working in sync to make it operate properly. It's quite amazing. "The human body has many parts, but the many parts make up one whole body. So it is with the body of Christ . . . . For just as each of us has one body with many members, and these members do not all have the same function, so in Christ we, though many, form one body, and each member belongs to all the others. We have different gifts, according to the grace given to each of us."[8] The *Expositor's Greek Testament* says the following regarding the above verse: "The One Body, of Many Members. The manifold graces, ministries, workings that proceed from the action of the Holy Spirit in the Christian community, stand not only in common dependence upon Him, but are mutually bound to each other. The Church of Christ is 'the body'. . . ."[9]

The Church is where our gifts function, and we need each other's gifts to complete us. One of the common illustrations of

---

7   1 Corinthians 6:19 NIV
8   1 Corinthians 12:12 NLT, Romans 12:4–6 NIV
9   *Expositor's Greek Testament,* https://biblehub.com/commentaries/1_corinthi-ans/12-12.htm

this truth is that of hot coals. If you put hot coals together, they get hotter and give off wonderful comforting heat that impacts the atmosphere around them. The coals feed off each other. However, if you take an individual coal and set it aside, even if it is red-hot, it will soon fade to lukewarm and eventually turn cold. Take that same piece of coal and put it back with the others and it gets hot again. In the same way, we as believers need each other, the Church.

After the apostle Paul had been shipwrecked with a band of prisoners on the island of Malta for three months and a mighty revival had taken place, they finally set sail for Rome. Along the way, they wintered on another island, then sailed again and came to yet another island. Paul was weary and worn. The Bible says he and his companion, Luke, immediately found brethren (the family of God) there and were invited to stay with them seven days. Word got out, and other brethren came to meet Paul. It says, "When Paul saw them, he thanked God and took courage."[10] Being with fellow believers brought courage to Paul and Luke. Yes, we need each other. We need the Church.

Love cannot exist in isolation. Grace cannot be received privately. Hope cannot develop in solitude. No gift or virtue can develop and remain healthy apart from the Church. Sin drives us into selfishness. Separation from God becomes separation from His people. The same salvation that restores us into relationship with God restores us into the community of the people of faith.

The life of faith is personal but is not meant to be individual. There is a family, a tribe, a nation, or a church. God's love and salvation are experienced fully in the congregation of His people. When God's people attempt to live in defiance to this truth, they become spiritually impoverished. When they submit to this truth,

---

10   Acts 28:15 NKJV, emphasis added

they flourish. Only when someone is planted into a house, into the soil of community, will they begin to thrive. There are times in life when, in our natural thinking, it seems better to isolate ourselves. In John's time, meeting together was like painting a target on their backs. It wasn't safe or convenient. Staying quiet and hidden would have been safer, but it is not God's way. So, with all of the above in mind, it comes as no surprise that John's vision on Patmos was not meant to be a private encounter simply to comfort him while on his miserable exile. God had a much bigger purpose. John was a mere vessel of God for the Church. This is how much God values His family. This is how important the Church is to His plans and purposes. It was for "the seven churches which are in Asia" (Rev. 1:4 NKJV). Just as the gospel pulls us into community, the Book of Revelation is for the household of God.

In Chapter 1, we saw that the opening words pronounce a blessing on the person who reads and those who listen and keep. It was understood that Revelation would be read and heard in the presence of believers. The idea that individuals would take the scrolls to read in the privacy of their own rooms was not even imagined. When John turned toward the voice that commanded his attention, the first thing he saw was "the seven golden lampstands . . . which are the seven churches" (v. 20 NKJV) to which he was the pastor. Then, in their midst, he saw the One "like a Son of Man" who was Jesus, the Christ. Christ is not seen apart from the gathered, listening, praying, believing, worshiping people. Equally, it is not possible to know the fullness of Christ and experience His best apart from His people. Sometimes we try. We would rather stay in our own little cocoon of spirituality, away from the organized body of believers. And it's no secret that family life gets messy at times. The Church is not for perfect people but is in many ways a hospital for the broken and wounded. It's a place where the Spirit of God inside living stones brings healing and comfort to His people.

There are times to receive healing and times to be conduits of healing. That's the body. Being involved requires risk, vulnerability, and a commitment that often interferes with our own personal structure. Unfortunately, many today want a Jesus who is goodness and truth but want to keep their distance from His family. What we end up with is a people who are hot after God but cool toward the Church. This has become a major issue in these last days. Even more so during the Covid-19 pandemic. It seems the enemy has used a virus to lock down churches and keep people in isolation. The enemy knows if he can isolate God's people, he can discourage and defeat many of them. One of his schemes then is to get them separated and away from the burning coals to cool them down. This is why the writer of Hebrews warns with urgency to "not [give] up meeting together, as some are in the habit of doing, but [encourage] one another—and all the more as you see the Day approaching."[11] The more we move into the end times, the more we are going to need each other. And I believe it's pretty obvious that we are rapidly approaching the Day.

But in regard to all of this the Son of Man says, "Write to the seven churches!" We would prefer to go straight from the awesome vision of Jesus in Revelation 1 to the magnificent worship in heaven of Revelation 4–5, and then onto the grand battle against the dragon in Revelation 12–14. However, to get there, we must go through the church and deal with those issues. And not just one church but *seven*. The church is that valuable to God.

As we read through the seven letters to the seven churches, we first see that they are identified geographically: Ephesus, Smyrna, Pergamum, Thyatira, Sardis, Philadelphia, and Laodicea. These

---

11   Hebrews 10:25 NIV

cities are located along a Roman postal circuit in modern-day Turkey. Each can be found on a map. Yet while the churches are located geographically, they are defined theologically by Jesus Christ Himself. The Ephesian church gets its identity from "him who holds the seven stars in his right hand and walks among the seven gold lampstands" (Rev. 2:1 NIV); the Smyrnan church from "the First and the Last, who died, and came to life" (Rev. 2:8 NKJV); the Pergamene church from "Him who holds the sharp two edged sword" (Rev. 2:12 NKJV); the Thyatiran church from Him who has "eyes like blazing fire and . . . feet . . . like burnished bronze" (Rev. 2:18 NIV); the Sardinian church from Him who "has the seven spirits of God and the seven stars" (Rev. 3:1 NIV); the Philadelphian church from "He who is holy, He who is true, 'He who has the key of David, He who opens and no one shuts, and shuts and no one opens'" (Rev. 3:7 NKJV); the Laodicean church from "the Amen, the Faithful and True Witness, the Beginning of the creation of God" (Rev. 3:14 NKJV).

Each of these churches, as well as all true churches today, are built on something apart from the identity of their geography and culture, namely, the resurrected Christ. Jesus is their identity, and it is He, through the working of the Holy Spirit, who builds the Church. The Holy Spirit of Jesus[12] breathes upon the chaos and makes a people His church. There is no true church apart from Jesus Christ and His power. Unfortunately, there are dead churches today. They have a "form of godliness but deny its power."[13] They are not built on the reality of the resurrected Jesus and His power. They are, as Craig Groeschel wrote, "Christian atheists."[14] They say

---

12   Philippians 1:19, Acts 16:7
13   See 2 Timothy 3:5.
14   Craig Groeschel, *The Christian atheist: Believing in God but Living as If He Doesn't Exist* (Grand Rapids, MI: Zondervan, 2010).

they believe but live as though Jesus is still in the grave. They don't actually believe the Bible is the infallible word of God and that Jesus literally rose from the dead. Yet everything about the Christian faith and the Church hinges on the reality of the resurrection. "If Christ has not been raised," wrote Paul, "your faith is futile; you are still in your sins."[15] The good news is, Jesus is risen! No longer in the grave, He is the victorious, glorified One that John saw on the Mount of Transfiguration and that appeared to him on Patmos as the Son of Man. Bill Johnson wrote in his book *Born for Significance*:

> This same John then saw Jesus sometime later in His glorified state in Revelation chapter 1. It was this John who wrote, "As He is . . ." Our life is patterned after the One who is raised from the dead, ascended to the right hand of the Father, and forever glorified. It almost sounds blasphemous to say, but our walk with Jesus is not patterned after His pre-glorified state. It is firmly established in the victorious Christ![16]

This is the Jesus that is empowering the true Church today through His Holy Spirit.

Both the apostle Paul and the apostle John wrote seven letters to seven churches. These seven churches represent all churches. As we've seen, each was located in a specific place and existed under the conditions of its geography, politics, and economics. At the same time, every church got its identity from the resurrected Jesus. However, while all churches get their identity from Him, each congregational identity is limited. No individual group reflects the entirety of Christ. Each one represents a piece of His essence. We

---

15   1 Corinthians 15:17 NKJV

16   Bill Johnson, *Born for Significance: Master the Purpose, Process, and Peril of Promotion* (Lake Mary, FL: Charisma House, 2020), 15.

can, however, be led to a place of wholeness as we listen to what "the Spirit says to the churches" and respond to Him in worship.

Throughout the Book of Revelation, one phrase is repeated again and again to the seven churches: "He who has an ear, let him hear what the Spirit says to the churches" (Rev. 3:22 ESV).Whatever differences there are between the churches, two things are constant: the Spirit speaks, and the people listen. The church assembles people to whom Jesus keeps His promises. For those promises to be complete, there must be listening ears attentive to the Spirit-spoken words. Listening is the common task of the church. Churches are listening posts, or centers. Listening is a spiritual act. Expensive equipment does not improve listening, it only makes hearing possible. "He who has an ear, let him hear what the Spirit says to the churches." From Genesis to Jesus the word is central, and therefore the act of listening is essential. Mouths speak so that ears may hear. "Morning by morning he awakens," wrote Isaiah; "he awakens my ear to hear as those who are taught. The LORD God has opened my ear, and I was not rebellious, I turned not backwards."[17]

So, in the Revelation on Patmos, John, in the Spirit on the Lord's Day, wrote the *seven* letters to the *seven* churches with expectation that each letter would be read aloud so that each church could hear what the Spirit was saying. In almost every case there was this judgment: "I have this against you." But in every case, there was an invitation to return and be restored. The judgment was never unto destruction. The judgment was always unto repentance and restoration.

Ephesus was the loveless church. The message was *"Return to Me as your first love"* (Rev. 2:4).

Smyrna was the persecuted church. The message was *"Don't be*

---

17   Isaiah 50:4–5 ESV

afraid" (Rev. 2:10).

Pergamos was the compromising church. The message was "*Change your ways*"(Rev. 2:16).

Thyatira was the corrupt church. The message was "*Keep the faith*" (Rev. 2:25).

Sardis was the dead church. The message was "*Wake up*" (Rev. 3:2-3).

Philadelphia was the faithful church. The message was "*Hold on*" (Rev. 3:11).

Laodicea was the lukewarm church. The message was "*Let me in*" (Rev. 3:20).

God's intention for the world is this: "I will be your God, and you will be My people."[18] This can only be fulfilled by those who are faithful to Him. It is God's will that we have a church. There is no evidence in ancient Israel or in the pages of the New Testament that churches were ever much better or worse than they are today. A random selection of seven churches in any century, including our own, would turn up something very much like the seven churches John pastored. So read through the second and third chapters of Revelation and see if you can find yourself. Then listen to what the Spirit is saying and respond to His invitation to return, to hold on, to keep the faith, to open the door of your heart and allow Him entrance.

---

18   2 Corinthians 6:16

THE LETTERS
David Binion, Dwan Hill, Krissy Nordhoff

He who has the ears to hear what the Spirit has to say
Speak Lord, speak Lord, speak Lord

Verse 1
You have been so strong
You have worked so hard
The striving and the strain
Won't take you very far
Return to Me, return to Me, My people, return to Me

Verse 2
You're wealthy, you have plenty
But you've endured so much
Just brave the accusations
Be faithful till you've won
Don't be afraid, don't be afraid, My people, don't be afraid

Verse 3
I know what you've done
I see where you've been
And I want you to know
This is not the end
Change your ways, change your ways, My people, change your ways

Verse 4
You had good intentions

Then you were led astray

So, tear down all the idols

And My love will remain

Keep the faith, keep the faith, My people, keep the faith

VERSE 5

Can you still remember

The visions and the dreams

Before the world had changed you

Before you fell asleep

Oh, wake up, oh, wake up, My people, please wake up

VERSE 6

I know your strength is fading

But you've been here before

You hold the key of David

That opens every door

So hold on, hold on, My people, hold on

VERSE 7

You've been in the middle

You can't decide what's true

I'm standing in the doorway

I won't force myself on You

(Will you) Let Me in, let Me in, My people, let Me in

Come Lord, come Lord, come Lord

Come Lord, come Lord, come Lord

Come Lord, come Lord, come Lord

Come Lord, come Lord, come Lord

7

COME UP HERE

Then as I looked, I saw a door standing open in heaven,
and the same voice I had heard before spoke to me like a trumpet blast.
*The voice said, "**Come up here**, and I will show you*
what must happen after this."

Revelation 4:1 NLT, emphasis added

Revelation Chapter 4 is the hinge of an open door elevated in heaven, inviting us to the more of God. There is such a place, you know. It's a place where we go to find more *of* Him, not more *from* Him. Just Him. Just in His presence. What's wonderful is when we find the more *of* God, we inevitably get more *from* God. It's just His nature to pour out and give to His children. Sadly, many, perhaps most, go to God with their petitions—bless this, provide that, protect me, guide me, show me, heal me. Even ministers find themselves more in love with ministry than simply Jesus. There is certainly a place for petition. We are instructed to go to the Father for all of our needs.[1] He wants us to ask as much as He wants to provide. It gives Him great pleasure. Yet there is a higher place. And when we come up higher, we experience the more of God and begin living from that higher place with Him. Author Mike Evans calls it living in the FOG—the favor of God.[2] Brother Lawrence called it practice of the presence of God. Watchman Nee described it as the communion of the Holy Spirit.

---

1   Philippians 4:6
2   Mike Evans, *Living in the Fog: The Favor of God* (TimeWorthy Books, 2013).

Throughout the entire Bible, there are invitations to a higher place. "Who may ascend into the hill of the LORD?" penned the Psalmist. "Or who may stand in His holy place? He who has clean hands and a pure heart, who has not lifted up his soul to an idol, nor sworn deceitfully."[3] A couple verses later in that chapter it says, "This . . . is what happens to God seekers, God questers."[4] The question is, Are you a God seeker, a God quester? He is a rewarder of those who diligently seek Him, and He Himself is the ultimate reward. Acts Chapter 17 has something profound to say about this: "And He has made from one blood every nation of men to dwell on all the face of the earth and has determined their pre-appointed times and the boundaries of their dwellings."[5] That is an amazing statement. Think of it. God designed the exact place in the course of mankind that we should exist. Where you are right now in time is exactly where you are supposed to be. Do you believe that? But why? Why did God put you here, at this point in time? The next verses tell us. "So that they should *seek the Lord*, in the hope that they might *grope* for Him and find Him, though He is not far from each one of us; for in Him we live and move and have our being."[6] Did you notice that word grope? One dictionary defined "to grope" as "feeling around with your hands in the dark trying to find a light switch."[7] Albert Barnes wrote in his 1870 commentary that "to grope" in this passage means "to search diligently . . . then to ascertain the qualities of an object by the sense of touch. And as the sense of touch is regarded as a certain way of ascertaining the existence and qualities of an object."[8] God created us to seek Him

---

3   Psalm 24:3-4 NKJV
4   Psalms 24:5 MSG
5   Acts 17:26 NKJV
6   Acts 17:27–28 NKJV, emphasis added
7   https://www.yourdictionary.com/grope
8   Barnes, Albert. "Commentary on Acts 17:27". "Barnes' Notes on the Whole Bible". https://www.studylight.org/commentaries/bnb/acts-17.html. 1870.

and to find Him, to grope for Him and ultimately to *touch* Him. But to touch Him, we have to reach up and look up—not inward into ourselves, not outward to others, but up to Him.

Isaiah writes that he saw the Lord, seated on His throne, "high and lifted up, and the train of His robe filled the temple."[9] The great monarchs and kings of history commonly wore long flowing robes as a symbol of strength and power. Imagine for a moment the most magnificent palace and a royal king sitting on his throne with dignitaries and servants gathered around him. Some seated, others standing, but all anticipating his words. Except this kingdom and throne is different from the others. The King's throne is raised up high, almost hovering, and the people are looking up. From His sitting position the train of the King's robe flows down and covers the entire palace, including every nook and cranny. All the people are under it like a blanket. Everyone is covered with the train of His robe. In heaven, the flowing robe is His presence. It is part of His being. His presence filled the temple. Isaiah saw God's presence.

That was in Chapter 6 of the Book of Isaiah. Thirty-four chapters later Isaiah is still inviting us to get up into the high mountain because he wants us to see what he was seeing, to behold our God. "O Zion, You who bring good tidings, get up into the high mountain; O Jerusalem, You who bring good tidings, lift up your voice with strength, lift it up, be not afraid; say to the cities of Judah, 'Behold your God!'"[10] What's interesting is Isaiah invited us up to the high mountain to behold God. Similarly, Jesus led John, Peter, and James up a "high mountain" to an elevated place where He could reveal Himself to them in His true glorified state. Have you ever wondered why He took them to a high mountain? Why didn't Jesus take them to some other secluded place? There were plenty in

---

9   Isaiah 6:1 NKJV
10   Isaiah 40:9 NKJV

that day. Maybe there was more to it.

Wanting us to have an elevated perspective, Jesus gives us another clue when He says, "Do you not say, 'There are still four months and then comes the harvest'? Behold, I say to you, lift up your eyes and look at the fields, for they are already white for harvest!"[11] Then the apostle Paul challenges us with the amazing truth that "God has raised us up together, and made us sit together in the heavenly places in Christ Jesus."[12] As stated earlier, I don't believe that Paul was simply describing what happens to us when we die. He was showing us that we also hold a place of honor and fellowship in heavenly places with Christ Jesus. But I'm convinced that many of our chairs remain empty in the House of God and in our hearts because we haven't understood this truth.

When Jacob dreamed about the gate of heaven in Genesis, with visions of angels ascending and descending, he declared, "Surely the LORD is in this place, and I did not know."[13] John painted a similar picture when he recorded Nathanael's encounter with Jesus. We examined this story back in Chapter 3 and saw that it's consistently believed by scholars that Nathanael was praying to God in complete solitude under the fig tree. That's why he was so astounded when Jesus told him, "Before Philip called you, when you were under the fig tree, I saw you." Nathanael knew no one could possibly have seen him pouring his heart out to God. Jesus continued, "You believe because I told you I saw you under the fig tree. You will see greater things than that." He then added, "Very truly I tell you, you will see 'heaven open, and the angels of God ascending and descending on' the Son of Man."[14] Nathanael had believed enough to pray but didn't realize that as he did, the door to heaven was swung wide

11 John 4:35 NKJV
12 Ephesians 2:6 NKJV
13 Genesis 28:16 NKJV
14 John 1:48 NKJV 50–51 NIV

open and Jesus was actually present. Isn't this true for so many people? They worship and pray and hope but don't actually believe He is watching and can be touched, that we can encounter heaven. The church has spent so much energy worshiping and serving from the earth toward the heavens, not realizing that we've been called to ascend the hill of the Lord and be seated in heavenly places and learn how to worship and serve toward the earth.

So, in this final book of the Bible, John sees an open door in heaven and hears the same voice that spoke to him before, saying, "Come up here, and I will show you what must take place after this" (Revelation 4:1 NIV). John's vision is consistent with the whole of Scripture in its invitation to this elevated position. And what he sees is breathtaking. His description is spectacular. He allows us to see and experience with him. But greater still, John is showing us the kinds of encounters that are possible with God and the man who will surrender his whole being in prayerful pursuit of the Lamb on the throne and remain faithful in spite of the trials and tribulation that might come. God still speaks. His old men dream dreams and His young men see visions. When God speaks, it's often to a people rather than an individual. When He calls for John to come up higher, He is also calling for all of us.

Over the past few years, I have begun to have divine visitations and encounters in my dream life, accompanied by elaborate Spirit visions. Sometimes the visions follow a dream. Something in the dream jolts me awake, but the vision continues as I awaken. Other visions occur while I'm driving. On one such occasion, I was driving the two-hour journey from San Diego to Los Angeles, completely swept up into a vision that lasted the entire drive. Upon my arrival I sat stunned by what I had seen and wrote it down. Only as I began the writing of this chapter did I realize the similarity to John's vision in Revelation Chapter 4. I will call it "The Dance."

9/15/17

I don't know how to describe what I see, but I'm captivated by the view. I behold a swirling flow of water, but not really water. It's "river-like" but unlike any river I've ever seen. Niagara comes to mind. A circling swirl of violent yet gentle love is being expressed, furious yet somehow calm and peaceful. At the center is a dance of passion between the Father and the Son. The most beautiful portrait of worship my eyes have ever seen. The Father eternally pouring His love out toward the Son. The Son eternally pouring out His love toward the Father. Endless love and devotion. Unmatched. Somehow there is another force drawing me, wooing me, romancing me. Inviting me to join the dance. But I can't. I'm not physically able to sustain what I see and live to tell it.

Somehow, however, I'm being drawn by an unseen force similar to the essence of the vision I'm seeing. The same essence, though unseen. I somehow understand that it is Him. A persona. The Holy Spirit. The Great Connector. Pressing me. Pulling me toward the torrent of passion between the Father and Son. Then it takes me, and I'm immersed. No longer seen yet seen. Visible but invisible. It was an enigma, an impossibility, a reality. And I look, I look . . . like Him. His image. Their image. They look the same. The Father is in the Son, and the Son is in the Father, and somehow I'm in the middle, beholding the most beautiful expression of love. And now I'm dancing. One with the Father and Son, drawn here by the Spirit. Surrounded by the Song and the Sound of Heaven.

The elders are there, casting their crowns. Beholding. Bowing. Angels crying. Holy, holy. Again and again. How can this be? I'm in the middle. In the midst. And they behold Him. But I'm here, and I discover there are others here. Dancing. We are all in Him, and He is in us. Dancing.

Then I'm suddenly back on earth, but somehow still in heaven. Heaven is not so far. Not as far as I always imagined. My heart is full of Him. Spirit. As I focus, I realize that I am wooing earth dwellers. Drawing, longing to bring others into the dance. We're all invited. My purpose discovered. Spirit. Inside of me. Pressing. Longing. I am His image. I feel I can command anything. I look like Him, so earthly things and heavenly beings respond to my command. Sickness, pain surrender to my declaration. But I'm on earth, yet still seated in heaven. Heavenly places.

Everyone come! Come up here! Come join me! Come join us! The Dance!

Psalm 65:9–13 in The Message paraphrase describes my encounter perfectly. "Oh, visit the earth, ask her to join the dance! Deck her out in spring showers, fill the God-River with living water. Paint the wheat fields golden. Creation was made for this! Drench the plowed fields, soak the dirt clods with rainfall as harrow and rake bring her to blossom and fruit. Snow-crown the peaks with splendor, scatter rose petals down your paths, all through the wild meadows, rose petals. Set the hills to dancing, dress the canyon walls with live sheep, a drape of flax across the valleys. Let them shout, and shout, and shout! Oh, oh, let them sing!"

I will ascend.

I will arise.

I will scale the mountain high. I've got a burning desire just for a look at You. I will ascend, I will embrace. I just want to see Your face. I will ascend the hill of the Lord. I just want to be with You.

COME UP HERE
David Binion and Mitch Wong

Chorus
Come up here
Come up here
Come up higher
Come up higher

Verse 1
I see the Throne
I see the One
As brilliant as gemstones
I see the glow
That swirls around
The brightest of rainbows
And from the Throne
A thunderous roar
And flashes of lightning
The seven flames
All stand ablaze
The Spirit's inviting

Chorus
Come up here
Come up here
Come up higher
Come up higher

Verse 2

The elders clothed
In whitest robes
With crowns that are golden
They all fall down
They cast their crowns
And worship before Him
Four beings rise
With wings and eyes
Magnificent faces
The great reprise
Both day and night
They all keep on saying

Tags

Holy, holy, holy is the Lord God Almighty
The One who always was, who is, and is to come

8

THE MIGHTY CHORUS

Worthy is the Lamb who was slain to receive power and riches and wisdom,
and strength and honor and glory and blessing!

Revelation 5:12 NKJV

After John ascends to the open door in Chapter 4, he witnesses
those amazing creatures crying, "Holy, holy, holy, Lord God
Almighty...," and the elders falling down before the throne, casting
their crowns and saying, "You are worthy, O Lord, to receive glory
and honor and power; for You created all things, and by Your will
they exist and were created" (Rev. 4:11 NKJV). Then, as John's
vision continues through Chapter 5, what does he witness? More
worship. The creatures. The elders. And this time the angels joining
in. "Then I looked, and I heard the voice of many angels around
the throne, the living creatures, and the elders; and the number
of them was ten thousand times ten thousand, and thousands of
thousands, saying with a loud voice: 'Worthy is the Lamb who was
slain to receive power and riches and wisdom, and strength and
honor and glory and blessing!'" (Rev. 5:11–12 NKJV).

A swirling, breathtaking experience, John is captivated by
this new revelation of worship. God wants to captivate us with a
revelation of worship too. It is one of the most life-giving revelations
we will ever have. When we pursue and practice true worship,
all heaven breaks out and we break through! John first sees the
inhabitants of heaven enthralled in extravagant worship numbering
in the thousands of thousands, but then every creature in heaven

and on earth and under the earth and everything in the sea joins in the great adoration.

Sandwiched between these two accounts of worship, John sees One seated on the throne holding a scroll in His right hand with writing on the inside and the back. A strong angel proclaims with a loud voice, "Who is worthy to open the scroll?" (Rev. 5:2 NKJV). When no one in heaven or on the earth is able to open it, John begins to weep, but one of the elders says to him, "Do not weep! See, the Lion of the tribe of Judah, the Root of David, has triumphed. He is able to open the scroll" (Rev. 5:5 NIV). However, when John turns to look at the Lion, however, he is shocked by what he sees. Instead of a lion, he sees a lamb that looks as though it has been slain. Things are not always as they seem. This Lamb that John sees is none other than the risen Christ who was crucified on the cross, the Lamb of God slain before the foundation of the world. William Barclay wrote concerning this verse, "The Lamb still bears the marks of having been slain. There we have the picture of the sacrifice of Christ, still visible in the heavenly places. Even in the heavenly places Jesus Christ is the one who loved us and gave himself for us."[1]

Next, as if in a scripted interdimensional play free from the grip of time, the slain Lamb before the throne breaks open the scroll and unveils a truth that sets in motion all of the events that would bring about the salvation of humanity. Heaven and earth erupt into explosive worship! "Blessing and honor and glory and power be unto Him who sits on the throne," the celestial beings proclaim, "and to the Lamb, forever and ever!" (Rev. 5:13 NKJV).

John, the pastor to seven churches in Asia Minor who were

---

1   Barclay, William. "Commentary on Revelation 5:6". "William Barclay's Daily Study Bible." https://www.studylight.org/commentaries/dsb/revelation-5.html. 1956-1959.

facing tremendous persecution and wicked political pressure, is now enduring his own cruel persecution. Instead of giving into despair, however, he prays and presses himself into the realm of the Spirit, where he beholds and discovers worship on another level. He finds that worship is the economy of heaven. Every exchange from heaven to earth and every response from earth to heaven uses the currency of worship.

Each time we come boldly before the throne of God with humble and undivided hearts in authentic worship, we tap into dimensions and dynamics of God's presence. We then are able to release His presence upon our lives—our families, our jobs, our finances, our daily routines. Worship is the highest posture a human can be in. We are our best when we're worshiping! We can only *give* honor, glory, power, and resources if we have them. Worship becomes the conduit for tapping into the Source and the Force of honor, glory, power, and the resources we need to accomplish God assignments. Worship moves the hand of God.

The Lamb before the throne reveals who He really is at the center of our worship. While the world is being tossed and torn in its values, while nations and generations are at war, God is looking to bring His kingdom of heaven to earth through worship. God does *not* want you under the yoke of this world. You are meant to be the head and not the tail! God wants you to reign in this life, NOW! When we worship, God works His plan in our lives. The mighty chorus is resounding eternally. We are invited to tap into the eternal sound and release the worship of heaven in the earth realm and see His kingdom come, on earth as it is in heaven. This is not John's encounter alone. This encounter is for all of us. When we worship on earth, both corporately and individually, heaven moves.

Not long ago I was leading worship at a conference in London. There were several services, and in one particular service the presence of God fell, and it became explosive. We worshiped for over an hour. After that, I released the band to leave the stage so we could get ready for the speaker. But the roar of worship coming from the congregation could not be stopped. It was fully alive. It roared and had a rhythm to it. Then bagpipes started playing over the speakers, followed by the cadence of a marching drum. I turned to acknowledge the musicians for stepping back up to facilitate this moment, but no one was there. I looked at the sound man thinking he was playing something, and he just shrugged his shoulders. Music from another dimension literally broke into our dimension and became one with the sound of worship rising from that room. It was breathtaking! It lasted for an hour. Then, like a vacuum, in an instant, the noise came to a stop, and not a sound was heard for another whole hour. It was a silence so profound you could almost feel it with your senses. The only movement was the constant stream of tears on the faces of the people. I am not embellishing here. I was there, as well as many others that can testify to the truth of this story.

Also, worshiping in the midst of our difficult and seemingly impossible circumstances stirs His presence to manifest, disrupting our environment, causing chains to fall off. Think about Paul and Silas. They were stripped, beaten, and thrown into the inner prison because of the testimony of Jesus, then locked in stocks. Stocks were restraining devices locked around the feet that kept the prisoners from moving. The inner prison was the deepest, darkest, most putrid dungeon. When they were thrown in, Paul and Silas weren't thinking they were getting out. They were thrown into that dungeon to silence them, but they wouldn't let the prison stop their song. They began to worship, and when they did, God's presence showed up in the form of an earthquake and shook that dark place to its foundation. Not only were Paul and Silas set free, but the chains binding every prisoner were broken and fell off.[2] My dad used to preach a sermon about this, and he would say he imagined Paul and Silas singing a song and God tapping His foot until He started to get up! All of the disciples were tortured in different ways to silence their voice, and then they were thrown in prison. John was no exception when he was tossed into a pot of boiling oil and then exiled on Patmos. He knew how to worship in the pain, isolation, and darkness.

I've been fortunate to witness God's presence manifest like this during a corporate worship service at a church. In the midst of worship, the glory of God came down, hit the room, and wrecked us. It was the most wonderfully terrifying experience. I climbed under the piano on my face. For five hours, I was under there, afraid to move. Yes. It's true. For five hours. I know it is hard to imagine in our instant cellphone culture. But I didn't want to move. I was thinking if I moved, I might mess things up, and I didn't want to be the one to quench the Spirit. Finally, I thought I should get up and sing, but I had no song appropriate for the weight of God's glory that was in the room. And I didn't even know that it had been five hours. Finally, I got up and looked at my watch. It was almost midnight. We had begun worshiping at six o'clock when the glory came. There was residue of that encounter at that property for three months.

My friend Max Davis, who helped me write this book, had a heavenly vision/encounter with worship strikingly similar to my vision "The Dance" I shared in the last chapter. Read about it in his own words:

"Two Olive Trees"

> First, what you have to understand is that this was more than a dream. It was at night while I was sleeping, but it was as real as anything I've experienced awake. I'm a journalist and hate

---

exaggeration so when I say it was more than a dream, believe me. In my entire life, I can count on one hand what I would consider God dreams. This was most definitely the top of the list. It was incredible. This would fall in the category of a God dream like Jacob had, or a night vision like Paul experienced. What you have to grasp is whether dream or vision, it was in high def and as real as anything I've experienced awake. It was incredible. I will never be the same.

I was standing in between two olive trees. Their branches were long and flowing, swaying back and forth in worship to God. The trees were actually worshiping! With my hands stretched upwards, I was worshiping along with them, swaying in sync with the branches. "More of You," I was repeating over and over. "More of You. More of You." Then, as I was caught up in exuberant worship, the two olive trees wrapped their branches around me like arms and hugged me. As they did, their leaves began to glow. Just like in the picture. The moment they started to glow, an explosion of divine love and peace burst through my body! I'm a writer and can't find adequate words to explain the intensity of love and peace I felt. It was the most incredible, wonderful, satisfying sensation I have ever felt. Nothing on this planet—no pleasure, no experience, no amount of money, no vacation, no thrilling football game—nothing even comes close. I would give up everything on this earth to be back in that moment. I long to go back one day. I will.

The whole time I'm between the glowing trees, my arms are in the air and I'm still saying, "More of You. More of You. More of You." That's all I said, "More of You," as God is pouring more of Himself into me until my human body could not take it any longer. Then, the two olive trees with me began to rise into the air. It reminded me of a hot-air balloon ride with the trees being the balloons. During all this, we never stopped worshiping. "More of You. More of You." As we rose, I instinctively knew we were going to heaven. When I looked down, I could see for miles and the landscape was definitely not south Louisiana. It was Israel! Then, I noticed on the horizon hundreds, maybe thousands, of other trees with people between them worshiping. It reminded me of a hot-air balloon festival. All rising towards heaven. At that point, I heard angels blowing the most beautiful trumpets, except the angels weren't just blowing trumpets, they actually were trumpets! They weren't playing instruments. They were celestial instruments. Just as we were about to enter into the next heavenly realm, I was brought out of it and woke up. I was very disappointed to come back but grateful for the glimpse of heavenly worship. My wife was next to me as it was happening. She thought I was dying but I was more alive than I have ever been! Later, I read in Revelation 11:4 about "the two olive trees and the two lampstands." That was kind of neat because I had no prior knowledge of that.

As I stated earlier in this book, my mandate, my earthly assignment, as a worshiper and a worship leader is to woo and draw others into the dance, of the mighty chorus. Every creature in heaven and earth is part of the song and the sound of heaven.

THE MIGHTY CHORUS
Revelation 5
Mitch Wong and David Binion

VERSE 1
Weep no more
For He has won
Lamb of God
The Worthy One
Join the sound of many thousands
Of ten thousand times ten thousand

CHORUS
Worthy is the Lamb who was slain
Worthy is the Lamb who was slain
To receive power, riches, and wisdom
Worthy is the Lamb who was slain
Worthy is the Lamb who was slain
Worthy is the Lamb who was slain
Strength and all honor, glory and blessing
Worthy is the Lamb who was slain

VERSE 2
Every tribe
And every tongue
Earth and heaven
Everyone

Join the sound of many thousands

Of ten thousand times ten thousand
Hear the Mighty Chorus resounding

BRIDGE
Blessing, honor, glory, power
Be to the One who sits on the Throne
Blessing, honor, glory, power
Be to the One who sits on the Throne
Blessing, honor, glory, power
Blessing, honor, glory, power
Blessing, honor, glory, power
Unto the Lamb forever and ever
Amen

9

THE ONES

After this I looked, and there before me was a great multitude
that no one could count, from every nation, tribe, people and language,
standing before the throne and before the Lamb. They were wearing white robes
and were holding palm branches in their hands.
And they cried out in a loud voice: "Salvation belongs to our God,
who sits on the throne, and to the Lamb."

Revelation 7:9–10 NIV

In the verses that lead up to the ones above, John hears a loud voice behind him saying that 144,000 servants of God, all from Israel, are destined to be sealed. This seal marks them as His witnesses and protects them from His wrath during the Great Tribulation. The voice further identifies them as twelve thousand from each of the twelve tribes. When John turns around, however, instead of seeing 144,000 people from Israel, he sees a crowd so vast that it's innumerable, representing every people group in the world (Rev. 7:4–8). Once again, we are faced with a duplicity in what John is seeing. Just as he had heard the Lion and turned to see the Lamb, and as the seven churches in his vision represent all churches everywhere throughout time, what John *sees* reveals the truth of what he *hears*: The number 144,000 is not *only* an exact count of the witnesses in the Great Tribulation period but also a symbolic number representing *all* people in time who are marked for God. The 144,000 people are marked as witnesses, but that doesn't mean that out of the billions of people that have ever lived, they are the only ones marked. All believers throughout time are marked witnesses. If we are in Christ, marked with His blood, we are His witnesses.

At the first Passover, the children of Israel, enslaved in Egypt, were instructed to apply the blood of a lamb on the doorposts of their homes. This not only marked them as belonging to Yahweh but also marked them for His protection. When the death angel was sent to destroy the firstborns throughout the land, the houses that were marked with the blood were passed over. In the same way, when we apply the blood of the perfect Lamb of God to the doorposts of our hearts, we become marked for Yahweh God, and His wrath passes over us. We are protected and sealed for eternity with Him. "O death, where is thy sting? O grave, where is thy victory?"[1] Jesus, the Lamb of God, was slain and rose again. This was a game changer. The Lamb, the Lion of the tribe of Judah, the Son of Man, is in heaven, a very real place, and we were raised up with Him and are seated with Him in the heavenly realms.[2] We also are His marked witnesses on earth. Many students of Revelation get hung up on whether the 144,000 is literal or symbolic. Actually, it's both. People get so distracted and hung up on the mark of the beast, 666, and what it is—a tattoo, a card, an implant. But what is even greater is that the Book of Revelation tells us that all the people of God are marked—tattooed and implanted with His blood! We must be careful to not have more faith in the Antichrist than we have in Jesus Christ.

There is an interlude between the sixth seal in Revelation Chapter 6 and the seventh seal in Chapter 8. It is an opportunity in time and eternity for people from every nation to receive His mark and take their place among the redeemed. God materialized

---

1   1 Corinthians 15:55 KJV
2   Ephesians 2:6

into eternity a momentary epoch called time. Humans were placed in the epoch of time, each in their assigned places with a life as a vapor.[3] The purpose is to be given the opportunity to seek Him, receive His mark, and become part of God's family, the body of Christ. Like a finger being pulled out of water and the hole disappearing, at some point this brief moment called time will be closed and swallowed by infinity.

Those billions of people around the throne from every nation and group that John turned and saw are the ones who have come out of great tribulation, not necessarily *the* Great Tribulation. Tribulation can mean seven years, but it could also be life in general. Every generation has faced tribulation, and most Christians experience some tribulation. After all, Jesus said to His disciples and to all believers, "In the world you will have tribulation; but be of good cheer, I have overcome the world."[4] That's a promise, but not one most have framed and hung on their walls! It really is comforting, though. If we are marked for Him, whatever happens— live or die, rich or poor—we can have peace and joy and be empowered as overcomers.

It's not a popular subject, but throughout history Christians have been martyred in all sorts of horrific ways. People are still being martyred today for Jesus in record numbers. My good friend Bishop Garlington told me, "I could take you to places in Africa where people have been macheted to death for their faith. We in America don't even understand that kind of tribulation. We've gone through some things, but we have not had to hide underground, like the church in China with the threat of imprisonment." Since the birth of the church when Jesus ascended, there has been an attempt of the demonic realm to silence its voice and influence, but

---

3   James 4:14, Acts 17:26
4   John 16:33 NKJV

the true church just keeps moving. That's because it's a God thing and the gates of hell will never prevail against it.[5] In fact, history has shown that the more persecution and tribulation, the more the church grows. "The blood of the martyrs is the seed of the church," wrote second-century church father Tertullian. While this is true, there is also a dark, painful side to persecution.[6] No one wishes for tribulation. Most of the freedoms we enjoy as Americans are a direct result of our Christian heritage, and we should never apologize for that. Where Christianity prevails, freedom always follows. Still, persecution and tribulation are a reality that should never dissuade us. The point is, we *can* overcome and not lose our faith in the midst of tribulation, as those who overcame "by the blood of the Lamb" (Rev. 12:11). One of the main points of this chapter, looking through a slightly different lens, is that there is hope for those going through tribulation. Jesus' message through John to the church is still don't give up. even when you are being persecuted. They may take your breath, but they can never take your eternal position with God.

After John turns and sees the billions of people marked by God, instead of 144,000, what does he see? Worship. More worship. All of God's people from every tribe and nation declaring, "Salvation belongs to our God who sits on the throne, and to the Lamb!" (Rev. 7:10 NKJV). We can't get distracted by the numbers of people and lose sight of the One seated at the center enthroned by worship. In the next few verses, 11–17, we see even more worship around the throne—angels, elders, creatures, along with those in white robes who came out of the Great Tribulation and were washed in the blood of the Lamb. All falling on their faces. But then listen to this verse: "He who sits on the throne will shelter *them* with his presence. 'Never again will they hunger; never again will *they* thirst. The sun

---

5   Matthew 16:18
6   https://www.sat7uk.org/does-persecution-truly-bring-church-growth/

will not beat down on them,' nor any scorching heat. For the Lamb at the center of the throne will be *their* shepherd; 'he will lead them to springs of living water.' 'And God will wipe away every tear from their eyes'" (Rev. 7:15–17 NIV, emphasis added).

Who are *they*?

The ONES.

These are the ones who have come through the Great Tribulation and all of life's tribulation. They are the ones that held on, the ones that didn't give up. They are the ones that are made overcomers by the blood of the Lamb. They are you and me.

THE ONES
David Binion and Mitch Wong

Verse 1
These are the ones who have come out of great tribulation
The ones who have washed their robes white in the blood of the
Lamb
A gathering of people so vast that no one could number
These are Your daughters and sons
These are the ones

Chorus
Salvation belongs to our God
Who sits on the throne
Salvation belongs to the Lamb
Salvation belongs to our God
Who sits on the throne
Salvation belongs to the Lamb

Verse 2
We are the ones who will join in the great celebration
We gather from every land, every tribe, every tongue
To offer You hallelujahs with voices of thunder
We are Your daughters and sons
We are the ones

Bridge
We overcome by the blood
And the word of our testimony

We overcome by the blood
And the word of our testimony
We overcome by the blood
And the word of our testimony
We overcome by the blood of the Lamb

10

SILENCE IN HEAVEN

When he opened the seventh seal,
there was silence in heaven for about half an hour.

Revelation 8:1 NIV

There was silence in heaven for about half an hour. Two things stand out in this statement: the word silence and the measurement of time, "about half an hour." Let's address the latter first. When John says there was silence in heaven for about half an hour, he's describing events in terms that he understands. He's on the earth living in a dimension where time is measured in seconds and minutes that turn into hours and days that turn into weeks and months that turn into years and generations. This physical earth is rotating on its axis while rotating around the sun. The sun is rising and setting, tides are coming in and going out. Growth and aging are occurring, marking the passage of time. Scripture tells us, however, that with the Lord, in His dimension, one day is not twenty-four hours but like a thousand years, and a thousand years like one day.[1] In other words, God doesn't measure time like we do. He views things from an eternal perspective. The formal definition of eternity is "a state to which time has no application; timelessness." If heaven is in a timeless, eternal state, how then are we supposed to calculate the meaning of "about half an hour"? John even says "about" because he's not entirely sure. In his

---

1   2 Peter 3:8

remarkable book, *Imagine Heaven: Near-Death Experiences, God's Promises, and the Exhilarating Future That Awaits You*, best-selling author and pastor John Burke talks about this very thing:

> *What will time be like in heaven? . . . Some [NDEers] describe it as timelessness, others note that there is a sense of time, but not in the same one-dimensional way we experience it on earth. And we see this indicated in Scripture as well, that time in heaven does not equate with our linear time, yet time can be experienced in heaven. John noticed time in heaven.* "When he opened the seventh seal, there was silence in heaven *for* about half an hour . . ." (Revelation 8:1, emphasis *mine). So even though a day in heaven may be like one thousand earthly years, there still seems to be the ability to experience some measure of time.* "It seemed as though I experienced so much in such a small length of earthly time. . . . Both time and space in earth stopped completely. Simultaneously, 'the time and the space' on the other side was completely alive, evident, and real. . . . While I was in the light, I had . . . [no] sense of time as I know it here on earth. In other words, no sense of the serial nature of time . . . past, present, or future. All times (past, present, and future) were experienced at every moment in time while I was in the light."[2]

Regardless of how time is measured in heaven, or if it is at all, what is sure is that the length of time in Revelation 8:1 is not what's crucial but what is taking place. It is something so important that it silences all of heaven.

After the seventh seal is opened, a crescendo has been reached and God halts every angelic expression, every whisper, every song. The elders surrounding the throne crying "Holy, holy, holy"

---

2   John Burke, *Imagine Heaven: Near-Death Experiences, God's Promises, and the Exhilarating Future That Awaits You* (Grand Rapids, MI: Baker Books, 2015), 130.

are hushed momentarily. The very idea is staggering. "Shhhhh! Silence!" as the hand of God is raised to draw attention away from the majestic worship that is continually rising before the throne. A divine "hush" from the mouth of the Supreme One so absolute it's like floating in open space beyond the earth's atmosphere, a celestial quietness, a stillness that we can't wrap our human minds around. Amidst the silence, heavenly ears are poised, listening, waiting to hear. But what? What would be important enough to make God pause?

Then, as if on cue, another angel steps up with an empty golden censer in his hand and stands at the altar. "He was given much incense to offer, with the prayers of all God's people, on the golden altar in front of the throne. The smoke of the incense, together with the prayers of God's people, went up before God from the angel's hand" (Rev. 8:3–5 NIV). Evidently, all the prayers of every generation since man first began to call on the Lord have been captured and saved. What do these prayers look like? Only heaven knows, but God has been collecting them.

On earth the high priests, such as Aaron, burned the censer full of incense before the altar in the temple or tabernacle. The sweet-smelling smoke represented the people's prayers ascending to God. Again, we see the duality in John's vision. The burning of incense by the priest in the earthy temple was a mere likeness of the reality in heaven where the smoke of the incense mixed together with the prayers of the saints and went up before God. After the offering before the throne in heaven, the angel took the censer filled with fire from the altar and hurled it through space and time, where it landed on earth. Upon impact there were "peals of thunder, voices, flashes of lightning and an earthquake" (Rev. 8:4–5 NIV).

Don't be fooled. Our prayers have impact. Prayers last forever. My mom and dad were praying people, as I mentioned before. They are in heaven today with all those who have died in the faith.

But every prayer they ever prayed was collected with all the rest. They still hold influence in heaven. All the prayers they ever prayed for me still hold weight. The fervent prayer of a righteous man or woman avails much.[3] It's just that God's time is not ours. The enemy wants us to think that our prayers don't matter, that they are landing on deaf ears. Jesus taught that we "should always pray and not give up."[4] Paul urged us to "continue earnestly in prayer."[5] He added that Epaphras was "always wrestling in prayer for you."[6] Sometimes prayer is wrestling, but God hears and collects them all, and in due time those prayers explode with potency and power! Fervent prayer gives us access to an environment in the heavenly realm where God is the center of all. John knew this and pressed into the Spirit in prayer even while on his personal Patmos. Yes, God hears every whispered plea, every groan and cry of brokenness, every intercession for revival in the nations. Don't lose hope in the silence. Every spoken syllable matters to Him. At the precise moment, the angel will hurl toward the earth divine answers that will shake the planet.

Silence in heaven shows that God listens. He pays attention. Face it, we live in a noisy world, surrounded by the clamor of cell phones chirping every minute with urgent messages for us, TVs blaring, cars and trucks roaring, sirens sounding, airplanes flying overhead, lawnmowers and Weed eaters whirring. We need headphones to block out distractions, but then we usually pump in loud music. Music is great but can also be a distraction. In a world overwhelmed by noise, we don't understand the power of silence and listening. Prayer, however, pierces through the noise and reaches the throne room of heaven. God hears and God listens. He listens! His listening is as great a wonder as His speaking to us. How often have we become

---

3   James 5:16
4   Luke 18:1 NLV
5   Colossians 4:1 NKJV
6   Colossians 4:12 NIV

completely hopeless, unable to find anyone who will listen? It is a rare thing to find someone, anyone, who understands everything we say. Every prayer we utter is heard and taken seriously.

Now, I'll be the first to admit, I don't know what that looks like or the mechanics of it all. He is God, omnipresent and omnipotent. I am not. A friend of mine told me a story about his close personal friend, an incredibly intelligent engineer, who was tragically struck by an eighteen-wheeler. He died on the spot and his spirit left his body. As it did, he encountered a magnificent angel who showed him parts of the eternal realm, which included unlimited dimensions. Unlimited. Think of that. Our brains start to crack trying to grasp just four dimensions! Finally, he cried out to the angel, "Stop! I can't take anymore," and he was brought back into his body. My point in this story is that something bigger than we can comprehend is going on. When Scripture says God gathers our prayers and is listening, though we don't understand it, we can count on it.

I know, know. I can hear some of you saying, "It sure doesn't feel like God's listening. Honestly, it feels like my prayers are bouncing off the walls, certainly not going to the throne of heaven! The only silence I hear is God not answering." All too often we relate to C. S. Lewis when he wrote in his classic book *A Grief Observed*:

> *When you are happy, so happy you have no sense of needing Him, so happy that you are tempted to feel His claims upon you as an interruption, if you remember yourself and turn to Him with gratitude and praise, you will be—or so it feels—welcomed with open arms. But go to Him when your need is desperate, when all other help is vain, and what do you find? A door slammed in your face, and a sound of bolting and double bolting on the inside. After that, silence.*[7]

---

7   C. S. Lewis, *A Grief Observed* (New York: HarperCollins, 1961), 5-6.

I will readily admit, along with C. S. Lewis, that the silence of God does at times seem loud. But all this about incense in heaven before the throne being the prayers of the saints is not just a bunch of religious mumbo jumbo. It's real. Heaven is real. God is real. Though we can't understand it all, it is real.

Back on earth, some two thousand years ago, yet outside of time and before the foundation of the world, fully present in the now, Jesus, the Lamb of God, died and rose again.

As I said previously, everything in the church hinges on this fact. Either He rose or He didn't. And as individual humans we must decide for ourselves. Don't get me wrong. I'm not saying that not believing means it didn't happen. He did rise and is alive and we must come into alignment with that truth. Doing so affects how we pray and expect and deal with seeming silence. The apostle Paul wrote to the church that if Jesus did not rise from the dead then his preaching was in vain, their faith was useless, they were still in their sins and to be pitied among all men because they were foolishly wasting their lives. Paul also said that if Jesus didn't rise then He and all the disciples, including John, were false witnesses of God because they all claimed they saw Him alive again. In other words, they would be liars, and worse, they would be liars about God![8] Think about it. Paul's whole life changed because of his encounter with the risen Jesus on the road to Damascus. There was a bright light that blinded him and a voice. Sound familiar? Paul endured beatings, imprisonment, shipwrecks, ridicule—you name it—and eventually laid his head on the guillotine. Every one of the disciples' lives changed because they saw the risen Jesus. All were martyred, and all they had to do to avoid the torture and death was say "I didn't see Him." That's it. John too wrote a testimony similar to Paul and

---

8   1 Corinthians 15:14–19

Peter's: "That which was from the beginning, which we have heard, which we have seen with our eyes, which we have looked at and our hands have touched—this we proclaim concerning the Word of life."[1] That's why in the midst of persecution, time on Patmos, and the seeming silence of God, John still prayed and pressed into His presence. He knew Jesus was the Son of Man risen and in heaven. Jesus risen changes everything. It means He is fully present whether we feel it or not, that He is listening whether we feel it or not, that we can have peace and be of good cheer while the storms rage around us.[2] John knew all of this. He wrote about it! It means that our prayers will eventually explode! There is a reason for the silence. God often speaks loudest in our silence.

When the Lamb cracked open the seventh and final seal, a great silence filled all of heaven, penetrating everything for about half an hour. Prayers were released. Prayer is access to an environment in which God is the center, where He stops everything and leans in to hear.

---

1   1 John 1:1 NIV
2   John 16:33

THESE THINGS MUST HAPPEN

So I went to the angel and asked him to give me the little scroll.
He said to me, "Take it and eat it. It will turn your stomach sour,
but 'in your mouth it will be as sweet as honey.'"

Revelation 10:9 NIV

Let's face it. The Book of Revelation is too immense to fully grasp everything that is revealed. As we have clearly seen, our limited minds can't comprehend the eternal perspective and imagery. No mere individual gets it all or can tell it all. Still, there are times we must speak what we do know and not hold back. There is something that can be said and needs to be said even if that means much of what we say is only in part. The apostle Paul acknowledged this when he said, "For we know in part and we prophesy in part. But when that which is perfect has come, then that which is in part will be done away."[3] Prophecy has to do with speaking. The "prophecy" that Paul is taking about here is speaking the things that God has revealed to us. When he says, "We prophesy in part," he is saying, "We speak what God has revealed to us." However, until we meet Jesus face to face—that which is perfect— our knowledge will be incomplete. Regardless of how well we speak on this earth, it will be an abbreviated version of the Word made flesh. That doesn't mean our inadequacy should exempt us from speaking what we can.

---

3   1 Corinthians 13:9–10 NKJV

What does all this have to do with Revelation Chapter 10? When John was told to eat the scroll, he was told what to expect. It would be sweet as honey in his mouth, but once it landed in his stomach and began to digest, it would become sour and bitter because he would be told to speak the prophecy, and many would reject it (Rev. 10:9–10). This is often the case with prophecy. Many times it is sweet as honey going down. Everybody wants a rhema word. Prophesy to me! People will travel across the country to conferences and meetings in hopes of getting a "word from God." Then they get one and often it's not what they want to hear, or it deals with something deep in their life that stings or becomes bitter. God reveals things to them so they can be dealt with. Ultimately, in prophetic words God wants to bring healing and freedom, to break every chain. God's intention is always healing, restoration, and redemption, even if it is painful at first. Prophecy, eating the scrolls that God gives, is kind of like a pregnant woman. The seed (Word) is received and conceived, but then as the Word starts to grow and do its work, there's a little bit of toilet hugging and eventually labor pains. But then a beautiful child is birthed, and the pain is forgotten. So it is with prophecy. Paul told Timothy, "This charge I commit to you, son Timothy, according to the prophecies previously made concerning you, that by them you may wage the good warfare."[4] Prophetic words in our lives often involve warfare and battles. They involve birthing. Ask any mother in the heat of labor and she'll tell you that birthing a baby is akin to war! But you keep pushing forward because of the promise that is the child. Birthing God things in us requires fighting and labor. Why do you think one of Satan's big strategies is abortion? He knows if he can stop life in the womb, he can stop a generation of souls that may receive and develop God's Word. There is a spiritual abortion where the enemy

---

4   1 Timothy 1:18 NKJV

wants to kill the prophetic inside of you. One minister said, "Satan wants to steal the prophetic word God gave you." John Calvin wrote concerning Paul's admonishment to Timothy:

It is as if he had said, "O Timothy . . . remember that thou art armed by divine prophecies for cherishing assured hope of victory and arouse thyself by calling them to remembrance. That warfare which we maintain, having God for our leader, is a good warfare; that is, it is glorious and successful.[5]

The most powerful work of a prophetic word happens after you've received it, then when it starts to do its work, you often wish you had never received a word! But let the sure word do its work. Fight for it! Then prophesy again as you wage spiritual warfare. My friend Phil Munsey said it like this:

PropheSAY it.

PropheSEE it.

PropheSEIZE it!

This is the heart of true prophecy. In John's vision about taking the scroll and eating, the prophecy would be sweet at first, but then reveal some dark things that are coming on the earth that would be rejected by many. John was told to speak even though he did not have full knowledge. He would have to wage warfare. Receiving this word, this Revelation, then delivering it would not be easy. But he must obey and speak even if he only understands in part, even if it might be rejected. "Then I took the little book out of the angel's hand and ate it, and it was as sweet as honey in my mouth. But when I had eaten it, my stomach became bitter. And he said to me, 'You must prophesy again about many peoples, nations, tongues,

---

5   John Calvin's Commentaries, Text Courtesy of Christian Classics Etherial Library, https://biblehub.com/commentaries/calvin/1_timothy

and kings'" (Rev. 10:10–11 NKJV). However, God's heart is still ultimate freedom and deliverance for the world and His people. This will become more evident in future chapters. It's important to note that while the dark details, prophecies, and overwhelming images in the Book of Revelation are significant, we can't get so distracted by the dark that we miss the light, the greater picture of God's love and unfolding plan of redemption. The Book of Revelation is no more about the beast and the dragon than Genesis is about the serpent. They are present, but they are not the central theme. Grace has to be the backdrop for the Book of Revelation. It's still all about Jesus and Him being the Word made flesh making a way for lost and doomed mankind when there seemed to be no way. We were lost and broken and were His enemies with no hope. The Book of Revelation is about bringing ultimate restoration and healing to the universe. Something bigger is going on. "Oh, taste and see that the LORD is good," wrote the Psalmist; "blessed is the man who trusts in Him!"[6]

An Important Warning

In Revelation 10:4 it says, "Now when the seven thunders uttered their voices, I was about to write; but I heard a voice from heaven saying to me, 'Seal up the things which the seven thunders uttered, and do not write them'" (NKJV, emphasis added). Writing in this case can be equal to speaking. Can you keep a secret? Sometimes God will ask you to "hold your peace." Not everything we get from God is meant to be shared. What secrets has He given you that will remain between you and God? Unlike John, when Paul was caught up to Paradise, he "heard inexpressible words, which it is not lawful for a man to utter."[7] In this case, he was told not to speak. We must be extremely careful when uttering the words,

---

6   Psalm 34:8 NKJV
7   2 Corinthians 12:4 NKJV

"Thus says the Lord" or "God told me to say . . ."

Yes, prophecy is often sweet going down, but if it's a real word it will do a work that one would almost regret. But we have to remember what God is doing in us and the world. It's all about freedom and healing and bringing us to more of Him, making us more like Jesus. We should worship and live in a way that "the Word is naked and open" to receive its mysteries. We can't just pick up the Bible and read it. We must let it read us. Then in that IN-TO-ME-SEE (intimate) sacred moment God reveals His secrets. You shall know the Truth! Worship always precedes prophecy. Therefore, prophecy must be held to through the night, until the Morning Star comes.

THESE THINGS MUST HAPPEN

Krissy Nordhoff, David Binion, Mitch Wong, Gracie Binion

Chorus

These things must happen
These things must happen
These things must happen, happen

Verse 1

The seven seals
And trumpet blasts
The seven bowls
Of holy wrath
The rise and fall
Of Babylon
Calamity
And martyrdom

A moon of blood
And falling stars
A multitude
That's set apart
A dragon rising
With a beast
Days of doom
And blasphemy

Chorus

These things must happen

These things must happen
These things must happen, happen

VERSE 2
The greatest army
ever seen
From far and wide
Will rise to meet
The King of Kings
And Lord of Lords
Riding on
The whitest horse

Armageddon will be won
By the Word
Of heaven's son
No more hunger
No more pain
No more darkness
Only day
These things

12

The seventh angel sounded his trumpet, and there were loud voices in heaven,
which said: "The kingdoms of this world have become the kingdoms of our Lord
and of His Christ, and He shall reign forever and ever!"

Revelation 11:15 NIV

I've always loved this passage of Scripture. Even as a teen with little understanding, I would feel the triumph in its declaration. "The kingdoms of this world have become the kingdoms of our Lord." Wow. How can you not get excited? Everything in this fallen evil world system is coming to its ultimate destiny. Every wrong will be righted. Every evil will be dealt with, all pain and suffering eliminated. Tears will be no more. We live on a planet broken and damaged because of sin. Satan has had free rein as the "god" of this world. Evil appears to be triumphing. Yet only for a season. To us it's a lifetime, but against the backdrop of eternity, our lifetime, even this earth age since the Garden, is like a speck of sand among the sands of every stretch of beach and every desert on earth combined. An ongoing theme in this book so far is our minds can't conceive of time without end. To be sure, it hurts God more than we can ever imagine seeing His creation suffer under the weight of sin and the enemy's destructive schemes. People cry, "Why does God allow pain and suffering?" The answer is, He did something about it! His strategy for dealing with the evil of this world system was to send His Son into the middle of it and to defeat it, to break the power of sin in the world, and to reconcile a people to Himself through Jesus. When Jesus hung on that cross and died, it appeared that evil had triumphed and Satan had won. But then, out of the ashes of defeat, God manifested His power and Jesus rose from the grave, conquering the power of evil and death once and for all. At the cross, the kingdoms of this world became the kingdoms of God. Now the reality of that victory is playing out in eternity and time when this earth will be healed and restored to its original state before the fall of Adam. This Book of Revelation reveals that.

This passage also reminds us of what Jesus taught us to pray: "This, then, is how you should pray: 'Our Father in heaven, hallowed be Your name, Your kingdom come, Your will be done, on earth as it is in heaven.'"[1] Instead of asking for it to happen, it's more an acknowledgment of what has already happened in the eternal realm and is manifesting on earth.

"Our Father in Heaven"

When we pray these words, we recognize that God is our Father. We name Him our Father. God created us in His image,[2] and every cell in our body was fearfully and wonderfully designed. It's in our DNA to worship and reverence Him, our blessed Creator. The majesty of God in creation and provision for us on the cross prompts us to praise as we ponder His ultimate love. "The Great, the Mighty God," penned Jeremiah, "whose name is the LORD of hosts."[3] When we come into His presence with prayer and praise, we bask in the blessed awareness of the all-knowing, all-powerful God establishing His kingdom in us and in the world.

"Hallowed Be Your Name"

His name is to be hallowed, or holy. "Holy, holy, holy is the LORD Almighty; the whole earth is full of his glory," wrote Isaiah.[4] These

---

1   Matthew 6:9–10 NIV
2   Genesis 1:27
3   Jeremiah 32:18 NKJV
4   Isaiah 6:3 NIV

words are repeated over and over in heaven before the throne of God (Rev. 4:6–8). This continual worship—giving glory and honor and thanks to the Lord in complete surrender—is offered up to God. The one who upholds us by His mighty hand is to be worshiped and honored above all things.[5] The kingdoms of this world have become the kingdoms of our Lord. Hallowed be Your name.

"Your Kingdom Come"

"Your kingdom come, your will be done, on earth as it is in heaven."[6] As I began to study the language of the kingdom, this idea took shape in my heart. When we pray, "Your kingdom come, Your will be done, on earth as it is in heaven," it's critical to understand that the way His kingdom comes to the earth is through His people. Jesus said, "For indeed, the kingdom of God is within you."[7] The apostle Paul added, "Christ in you, the hope of glory."[8] The kingdom is within reach. It's within our grasp. Thus, our prayer in life should be, "Lord, establish Your will *in* us, and then establish Your will *through* us. Help us begin to live out Your kingdom here on earth by being Your people, carrying Your presence and agenda everywhere we go."

We are a people Jesus called to be salt and light in the world.[9] Salt and light are as different as peanut butter and jelly, but they both have one thing in common: They change their environments. Likewise, with the kingdom of God within us, we are called to change our environments with His presence, bringing His kingdom to earth. This, however, requires a surrendering of our hearts and minds. It requires a heart of repentance. "Repent," declared Jesus, "for the kingdom of heaven is at hand."[10] In other words, the

---

5   Isaiah 41:10, 16
6   Matthew 6:10 NKJV
7   Luke 17:21 NKJV
8   Colossians 1:27 NKJV
9   Matthew 5:13–16
10   Matthew 4:17 NKJV

kingdom of heaven is closer than you think. It's right here, within reach. But we must repent. The word repent doesn't have to be scary or threatening. It simply means to change your mind or the way you think. The Apostle Paul challenges us not to "conform to the pattern of this world but be transformed by the renewing of your mind."[11] Conformity to the world and its kingdom takes no effort. It just happens naturally. But when we intentionally renew our minds by bringing them into alignment with the truth of God, something supernatural happens. We become transformed! Unless we allow the Spirit of God to change the way we think, we will never see the kingdom of God. Yet as we worship Him and dedicate our minds and thinking to His will and purpose for our life—His kingdom agenda—God will use us to build His kingdom.

One final thought. Because of the population explosion of the past two hundred years or so, the number of people on the earth right now is more than the previous six thousand years combined. They tell us that perhaps during the first thousand years since creation there were approximately one billion people on the planet. The same can be said for the second thousand-year period. And the third, and the fourth, and the fifth. And even the sixth. But experts tell us that there are now approximately eight billion people on our planet today. If these numbers are true, then we are nearing the tipping point, if we aren't already there. It could be said that there are now more Christians on earth than there are in heaven. Think of the impact we could have on the world for God's kingdom if we all allowed the Holy Spirit to flow through us uninhibited. It would be staggering.

---

11   Romans 12:2 NIV

HALLOWED

David Binion, Mitch Wong, Steffany Gretzinger, Madison Binion

Verse 1

Hallowed presence

Evidence of heaven

Manifest as we gather to worship Your name

Kingdom come to us

Will be done through us

Dwell with us, come establish Your kingdom today

Chorus

Just as it is in heaven

Just as it is in heaven

Let it be done here in the earth

Just as it is in heaven

Just as it is in heaven

Let it be done here in the earth, Lord, we pray

Verse 2

Keep us from temptation

Deliver us from evil

Forgiving us as we forgive others the same

Bread of Life feed us

Living Word lead us

Son of God, would you teach us to pray as You pray

Bridge

It's Your kingdom

And Your power

It's Your glory
Forever and ever, amen

KINGDOMS
David Binion and Mitch Wong

Verse 1
We thank You, O God
Who is and who was
You took Your power
And You took over

Verse 2
The time has arrived
It all comes to light
Your perfect judgment
Is all around us

Chorus
The kingdoms of this world
Have become the kingdom of our God
And His Messiah
O hallelujah
The elders and the saints
All Your servants glorify Your name
You reign forever
O hallelujah

Verse 3
The trumpets have played
No seals left to break
We join with heaven

Your people singing

Heaven's open
Heaven's open
Heaven's open
Here and now
See the lightning
Feel the thunder
Heaven's open
Here and now

13

SONG OF MOSES AND THE LAMB

They held harps given them by God and sang the song of God's servant Moses
and of the Lamb: "Great and marvelous are your deeds, Lord God Almighty.
Just and true are your ways, King of the nations. Who will not fear you, Lord,
and bring glory to your name? For you alone are holy. All nations will come and
worship before you, for your righteous acts have been revealed."

Revelation 15:2–4 NIV

Before we can fully understand what is happening in this
passage, we must first view it in context. Chapters 6 and 7 reveal
that six of the seven judgments are released after their seals are
broken. Once the sixth seal is broken, an explosion of worship
erupts around the throne. "And they cried out in a loud voice:
'Salvation belongs to our God, who sits on the throne, and to the
Lamb'" (Rev. 7:10 NIV). The angels were positioned around the
throne, attentive and upright, standing in the presence of the elders
and the four living creatures, but when the sixth seal is broken,
"They fell down on their faces before the throne and worshiped
God, saying: 'Amen! Praise and glory and wisdom and thanks and
honor and power and strength be to our God for ever and ever.
Amen!'" (Rev. 7:11–12 NIV).

It is between the sixth and seventh seal—the same interlude
we saw in Chapter 9—that this great moment of worship breaks
out. Revelation 8:1 is where the seventh seal is opened. When it is
released, the indescribable sound of the celestials worshiping around
the throne pauses and there is the half-hour of silence in heaven.

Following this holy moment of quiet is a second group of seven judgments as seven angels with seven trumpets prepare to sound them. There are so many sevens that my head is spinning! Let's take a quick moment to address the significance of this number before we move on. Clearly, seven is a meaningful number throughout Scripture, and particularly in the Book of Revelation, but that's a topic for a whole other book. Briefly, as most of us know, seven is God's number, representing His perfection and completion. The use of the number seven over fifty times in the Book of Revelation is clearly intentional: seven churches, seven golden lampstands, seven stars, seven lamps of fire, seven Spirits of God, seven seals, seven judgments, seven bowls, seven thunders, seven horns, seven eyes, seven mountains, seven heads, seven crowns, and seven kings. Perhaps by using the number seven, God is sending a message that He is perfecting and bringing His plan for the ages to completion and perfectly completing His church. God is number seven, and His hand is directing all of Revelation. He is sovereign and in total control.

Now back to the Song of Moses and the Lamb being sung in Revelation 15:2–4. The first six trumpet judgments are chronicled in Chapters 8 and 9, but it is not until much later, in Revelation 11:15, that the seventh angel sounds his trumpet. When this happens, great worship erupts in heaven yet again! "The seventh angel sounded his trumpet, and there were loud voices in heaven, which said: 'The kingdom of the world has become the kingdom of our Lord and of his Messiah, and he will reign for ever and ever.' And the twenty-four elders, who were seated on their thrones before God, fell on their faces and worshiped God, saying: 'We give thanks to you, Lord God Almighty, the One who is and who was, because you have taken your great power and have begun to reign'" (Rev. 11:15–17 NIV).

Then something unusual happens in Chapter 12. Verses 1–2 say, "A great sign appeared in heaven: a woman clothed with the sun, with the moon under her feet and a crown of twelve stars on her head. She was pregnant and cried out in pain as she was about to give birth" (NIV). Verses 3–4 add, "Then another sign appeared in heaven: an enormous red dragon with seven heads and ten horns and seven crowns on its heads. Its tail swept a third of the stars out of the sky and flung them to the earth. The dragon stood in front of the woman who was about to give birth, so that it might devour her child the moment he was born" (NIV).

The imagery throws us into a tailspin. We've got this seven-headed dragon showing up breathing fire and hate, threatening a pregnant woman having labor pains. What we've observed so far seems to be a chronological prediction of things to come in the last days. After that we are given this image of a terrifying muti-headed dragon that makes Godzilla look like an ant and is big enough to fling stars through the universe with its tail. This cosmic flying lizard is hellbent on killing the child. John here is giving us a whole different perspective of the nativity. When Jesus was born, and long before His birth, principalities and powers, led by this dragon, unleashed their efforts to keep Him from starting and completing His mission. On earth, in what's been called "the Massacre of the Innocents," Herod the Great, king of Judea, ordered the execution of all male children two years old and under throughout the areas around Bethlehem.[1] That was just one of many schemes of the dragon throughout history to stop the birth of the One that would eventually "crush his head"[2] and complete God's plan of redemption for the human race. The Old Testament is filled with examples of God's enemies trying to wipe out His chosen people,

---

1   Matthew 2:16–18
2   Genesis 3:15

Israel, in an attempt to stop the lineage of Jesus from happening. Yet God was always one step ahead with His plan in place from before the foundation of the world.

This dragon of Revelation 12 is also responsible for the fall of a third of the angels in heaven. Most scholars consent to this view. And now we are introduced to this seemingly misplaced depiction of the dragon attempting to kill the Christ Child. In verse 7 John gives us this detail: "Then war broke out in heaven. Michael and his angels fought against the dragon, and the dragon and his angels fought back." Verses 8–9 continues with, "But he was not strong enough, and they lost their place in heaven. The great dragon was hurled down—that ancient serpent called the devil, or Satan, who leads the whole world astray. He was hurled to the earth, and his angels with him" (NIV).

It seems that John is not writing about something that happens in the future. Rather, this is an accepted reality that took place thousands of years before. But the intriguing details go on in verses 10–11, bringing us "back to the future" with the statement, "Then I heard a loud voice in heaven say: 'Now have come salvation and the power and the kingdom of our God, and the authority of his Messiah. For the accuser of the brothers and sisters, who accuses them before God day and night, has been hurled down. They triumphed over him by the blood of the Lamb and by the word of their testimony; they did not love their lives so much as to shrink from death" (NIV).

Sandwiched between the seven seals and the seven trumpets sounded by the seven angels, the past and future converge like a quantum superposition of atoms occupying two spaces at once. Past, present, and future become one as time morphs into the eternal. We see a reflection of the past but at the same time jump to the final impending victory. Moving from there, the next two chapters give us a glimpse into the strategy and workings of the beast and the dark world of principalities and powers. Chapter 15 then circles us back to the beginning of this Chapter 13 and the Song of Moses and the Lamb. You get all that?

HARPS AND REWARDS

We are presented with the seven angels waiting to release seven final plagues. Yet before they are given the "go" signal, we see those who had been victorious over the beast and its image. They are standing by what looks like a sea of glass glowing with fire, holding harps given to them by God and singing the song of God's servant Moses and of the Lamb. Stop right there. Try to imagine holding a harp given to you by God. As a worshiper with a love for instruments, oh how I would love to get my hands on one of those! The best instruments on earth made by the most skilled craftsmen—a Stradivarius violin, a Martin guitar, a Steinway piano, or even the harp David played—can't come close to a harp personally given to you by the Creator of the universe. Plus, we will supernaturally have the skill to play! Once again, we see that Revelation weaves its way back to worship. It's amazing to me that one of the rewards for being victorious over the beast is worship. Worship is a reward! Between the rushing waters and the glowing olive trees is the greatest reward because we are entering the dance with Him.

And here in Chapter 15 is an Old Testament reference to Exodus where the Song of Moses was first mentioned after the children of Israel had experienced victory over their enemies in Egypt. The plagues were released in Egypt because Pharaoh refused to let Moses take God's people into the wilderness to worship. The prophetic implications are significant. We'll talk more about that in the chapter about the Fall of Babylon. In the meantime, here are the lyrics of the Song of Moses and the Lamb.

Great and marvelous are your deeds, Lord God Almighty.

Just and true are your ways, King of the nations.

Who will not fear You, Lord,

And bring glory to Your name?

For You alone are holy.

All nations will come and worship before You, for Your righteous acts have been revealed.[3]

After this song, the temple in heaven is opened. Out of the temple come the seven angels with the seven plagues. I propose that each of these series of plagues comes in cycles throughout history and will continue to be released in the future. Could we be seeing three different perspectives, much as the four Gospels give us different perspectives of Jesus' earthly ministry? Is John retelling the whole story of the Bible in one final capsulized book? Every story in the Old Testament points to Jesus, the Lamb. Every prophet of the Old Testament points to Jesus, the Lamb. It is consistent that this final Revelation point to Jesus, and it rightfully opens with the impossible-to-miss declaration, "This is the Revelation of Jesus."

---

3   Revelation 15:3–4 NIV

SONG OF MOSES AND THE LAMB
Mitch Wong and David Binion

Verse 1
Mighty and marvelous
All of Your miracles
Lord God Almighty
Righteous and true to us
Your ways are glorious
King of all the nations
King of all the ages

Chorus
Who will not fear with reverence and awe?
Who will not fear the Lord, the Lord?
Glory and praise to the Name over all
Who will not fear the Lord, the Lord?

Verse 2
Nations from far and wide
Coming to glorify
Yahweh, Yahweh
There will be no dispute
Your deeds reveal the truth
You alone are holy
You alone are worthy

BRIDGE
Let the temple be filled with Your glory
Your power and glory
Magnificent glory

14

HALLELUJAH, BABYLON HAS FALLEN

After this I saw another angel coming down from heaven.
He had great authority, and the earth was illuminated by his splendor.
With a mighty voice he shouted: "Fallen! Fallen is Babylon the Great!"

Revelation 18:1–2 NIV

"Fallen! Fallen is Babylon the Great!" Yes! Wonderful! Praise the Lord!

Wait a minute. What does that even mean? Who is this Babylon the Great that John is writing about? Could it be the proud and defiant Tower of Babel whose construction came to a screeching halt when God confused the languages of the workers and scattered the population? Or could Babylon the Great be the wicked and wealthy city of Babylon devoted to sensualism and materialism that was conquered along with the great Babylonian Empire? While these played a role to some degree, I would put a checkmark in the box labeled "None of the above." John wasn't really talking about either of those. He was referring to something much greater.

In short, throughout the Book of Revelation, "Babylon" is a metaphor, a word used with a long history that started with the story of the Tower of Babel. In fact, the word Babylon is derived from the word Babel. The story of the Tower of Babel is told in Genesis 11. After the flood, humanity was arrogantly seeking to rebuild the world without God . . . again. You'd think they would have learned from history. Do we ever? Unified, with one language, they started constructing what they deemed a great tower with the goal of piercing the heavens and boastfully declaring their greatness in the face of God. "Come, let us build ourselves a city, and a tower whose top is in the heavens; let us make a name for ourselves, lest we be scattered abroad over the face of the whole earth."[1] God wasn't amused. He just wiggled His celestial finger and confused their languages, causing them to divide into the different people groups so that humanity could not find its unity apart from Him. It was exactly the opposite of what they wanted. Man would never again be unified like that until the end days when the One World System is set up once again in a final attempt to overthrow God's plan.

There's an interesting contrast to Genesis 11 in Acts Chapter 2. Back in Genesis when man was united without God, He confused their languages and thus divided and confused their plan. In the Book of Acts God once again used unknown tongues. This time, however, it was to unite a people in their pursuit to bring God back into the center. Babel or Babylon is a clue to John's churches that he is referring to a people seeking to build society without God.

In Revelation Chapter 17, Babylon the Great was represented as a woman sitting on a blasphemous beast with seven heads that represented seven hills. "The woman was dressed in purple and scarlet, and was glittering with gold, precious stones and pearls. She held a golden cup in her hand, filled with abominable things and the filth of her adulteries. The name written on her forehead was a *mystery*: BABYLON THE GREAT, THE MOTHER OF PROSTITUTES, AND OF THE ABOMINATIONS OF THE EARTH" (Rev. 17:4–5 NIV, emphasis added). At that period in history, Rome was built on seven hills. The seven churches would

---

1   Genesis 11:4 NKJV

have understood that John was referring to Rome; however, the definition of Babylon is much broader. It is Satan's world system since the fall of man, built on pride and sin that attempts to build its kingdoms apart from God, both as individuals and nations. Mankind inherently wants to do his own thing independent of God. That is at the core of Babylon.

But let me cut to the chase and let the cat out of the bag. Babylon always falls. Even before creation, Lucifer exalted himself with pride and was thrown from the heavens. Jesus referenced this when He said to His disciples, "I saw Satan as lightning fall from heaven." Ezekiel 28 gives us a great description of this.

> *You were the seal of perfection, full of wisdom and perfect in beauty. You were in Eden, the garden of God; every precious stone adorned you: carnelian, chrysalises and emerald, topaz, onyx, and jasper, lapis lazuli, turquoise and beryl. Your settings and mountings were made of gold; on the day you were created they were prepared. You were anointed as a guardian cherub, for so I ordained you. You were on the holy mountain of God; you walked among the fiery stones. You were blameless in your ways from the day you were created till wickedness was found in you. Through your widespread trade you were filled with violence, and you sinned. So I drove you in disgrace from the mount of God, and I expelled you, guardian cherub, from among the fiery stones. Your heart became proud on account of your beauty, and you corrupted your wisdom because of your splendor. So I threw you to the earth; I made a spectacle of you before kings.*[2]

Proverbs adds, "Pride goes before destruction, a haughty spirit before a fall."[3] James reinforced this when he wrote, "God opposes

---

2   Ezekiel 28:12–17 NIV
3   Proverbs 16:18 NIV

the proud but shows favor to the humble."[4] Lucifer was the first example of this kind of fall. The people at Babel in Genesis 11 demonstrate again the kind of destruction that pride attracts.

You can see this thread throughout Scripture. Babylon always falls. David was anointed and established as the king of Israel to replace a proud Saul. But then even David slipped into a moment of pride when he instructed his leaders to do a census to number the men in Israel because he wanted to know the power of his own strength. God disciplined David because he placed his trust in the force of his armies rather than the hand of God, who had led him to great victories. All of the kings that followed David showed us the rise and fall of Israel again and again because of the men who would abandon their pursuit of Jehovah and turn to worship Baal. All of the prophets warned Israel to turn back to God or suffer their own destruction. Jeremiah, Isaiah, Ezekiel, and others declared that Babylon, the great nation, would overthrow the people of Israel and take them into captivity as punishment for their pride. For seventy years they endured hardship at the hands of Babylon and her leaders. Esther, Daniel, Ezra, and Nehemiah were all beacons of hope for the people during their exile, encouraging them to turn their hearts back to God. Eventually, God would send other nations to lay siege to the great city and nation of Babylon, completely destroying it and leaving it in ruins. But not before the Jews were released under the lead of Ezra and Nehemiah to return to Jerusalem and rebuild the walls of their beloved city.

But Babylon always falls.

So, let's get back to the Book of Revelation. Those of us living in the twenty-first century have interpreted this passage as some future event. Somehow the city and nation of Babylon will be rebuilt

---

4   James 4:6 NIV

so that all of the predictions given by John can come to pass. I don't believe that is necessarily the case. Saddam Hussein attempted to build a palace close to the ruins of the ancient city but did not succeed. And the ruins of the old city are barely recognizable. I believe that John was speaking to the people of his generation about their current state of affairs and encouraging them to never give up no matter how difficult things become. Blessed are those who hold on till the end! I believe for those people, John was referring to the domineering forces of Rome. So, the question remains, how does this speak to us today? The message is the same. The spirit of Babylon continues to infiltrate our world systems and seize control of our governments, entertainment spheres, school systems, and even the church. And the message to us is, no matter how hot the fire burns in the furnaces of influence, don't bow to their images! Don't give in to their philosophies. Hold on to the promises of God! Be encouraged, Babylon always falls!

I must bring this word of caution to the church. Beware of Babylon. She starts out subtle and creeps in slowly, learning our strengths and weaknesses. She has thousands of years of experience turning humble hearts to prideful ones by mixing partial truth with lies and deception. We've seen great men of God influenced by the spotlight of favor rise to heights in the eyes of men, only to succumb to the pressures of sustaining their own success and stumble into great sin before they realize the trap had been set. Babylon ultimately wants to humiliate the people of God and discredit our influence.

I am greatly concerned about what I see in the worship community. I am fully aware of the financial blessing that comes to some of the artists who lead God's people, and for those who write the music to facilitate those artists. I remember early in my writing career receiving my first royalty checks. I had no idea that this kind of money could be made. After my first successful song, my publishers began reaching out to me to write the next big song. My song was at the top of the charts, which meant two things: They were selling a lot of albums, and as a result I was getting heavy rotation at the radio stations. This gave me two streams of income that I never anticipated. I must admit, I was thrilled. But I found myself at a crossroads and had to make a decision. I was young at the time, but the presence of God was too precious to me to allow myself to be seduced by the money. I remember responding in my own heart and mind that my motivation to write the song that God was obviously blessing was never about the money. I was at the beginning of a life of worship and had to choose whether I would bow to the image of what others deem successful or stay true to my heart for the presence of God.

As worshipers, we have been invited to carry the glory but never touch it; to be close enough to bear the weight of His presence on our shoulders but never touch it with our hands and think that it belongs to us. I'm afraid today that the ark of God's presence has been covered with smudgy fingerprints by people desperate to make a name for themselves. Merchandising our ministries has become a big business. There is no ignoring when favor rests on an individual and their notoriety begins to skyrocket. I've known many seasons of great favor in my own life and know that it takes a lot of funding to produce the music that God is giving us. I believe in excellence, but I also believe in good stewardship. I'm not here to shame anyone or cast judgment, but please heed this warning: Beware of Babylon. Babylon always falls. Step into your season of favor and increase but proceed with caution. Surround yourself with people, pastors, and friends who will speak truth and hold you accountable.

Throughout the book of Revelation, John gives us a vision of great victory. We see the ultimate victory when the King of kings and Lord of lords returns with a great heavenly host to rule and reign. We anticipate that great day and long to see it. But Revelation isn't just about our future. It's also about our now. It encourages us to not give up while enduring tribulation. It encourages us with triumphant declarations when we hear "the kingdoms of this world have become the kingdoms of our God!" Can't you hear the militant overcoming declaration, "Hallelujah! Babylon has fallen! No more tyranny! No more crying! Hallelujah! God has spoken! Babylon has fallen!"[5]

---

5   My paraphrase

HALLELUJAH, BABYLON HAS FALLEN

Chorus
Hallelujah, Hallelujah

Hallelujah, Hallelujah

Hallelujah, Hallelujah

Hallelujah

Bridge
Babylon has fallen

Babylon has fallen, fallen

Bridge 2
Amen

READING REVELATION 19:6 (TPT)

6

Then I heard what seemed to be the thunderous voice of a great multitude, like the sound of a massive waterfall and mighty peals of thunder, crying out:

"Hallelujah!

For the Lord our God, the Almighty, reigns!"

7

"Let us rejoice and exalt him and give him glory,

because the wedding celebration of the Lamb has come

And his bride has made herself ready."

Chorus
Hallelujah, Hallelujah
Hallelujah, Hallelujah
Hallelujah, Hallelujah
Hallelujah

Bridge 2
Hallelujah, God has spoken
Babylon has fallen, fallen
Hallelujah, Hallelujah

15

KING OF KINGS AND LORD OF LORDS

I saw heaven standing open and there before me was a white horse, whose rider is called Faithful and True. With justice he judges and wages war. His eyes are like blazing fire, and on his head are many crowns. He has a name written on him that no one knows but he himself. He is dressed in a robe dipped in blood, and his name is the Word of God. The armies of heaven were following him, riding on white horses and dressed in fine linen, white and clean. Coming out of his mouth is a sharp sword with which to strike down the nations. "He will rule them with an iron scepter." He treads the wine press of the fury of the wrath of God Almighty. On his robe and on his thigh, he has this name written: KING OF KINGS AND LORD OF LORDS.

Revelation 19:11–16 NIV

It's interesting to note that the One called Faithful and True riding on the white horse is followed by His army, who are also on white horses and are clothed in white linen. Now nearly everybody knows that warriors don't wear white linen into battle, right? Helmets, tunics, swords, boots, body armor, yes, but clean white fine linen, not so much. Something else must be going on in this scene. In biblical times, kings and other royalty wore fine linen that was soft and smooth, akin to silk. More importantly, Aaron and all the high priests after him were required to wear garments made of fine linen in order to enter the Holy of Holies. It was a symbol of purity. "Fine linen stands for the righteous acts of God's holy people" (Rev. 19:8 NIV). In other words, these heavenly armies following their King of kings were clothed in righteousness!

And here's another interesting thing: They never actually had to fight in this frightening battle of the ages that they were riding into. The soldiers in linen never had to lift a sword or a finger. Their fine whites never got so much as a smudge. Why? Because when the King of kings and Lord of lords arrives, He strikes down the nations rising up against Him with the words of His mouth. With the brightness of His coming and the sword in His mouth, all of His enemies are destroyed. This is not a battle between two equals in strength. There is no contest. All of the dark resistance and evil influence that God's people have had to endure is shattered in an instant with just a word from the mouth of the One on the white horse.

"I saw heaven standing open." John is writing what he sees. He sees Jesus. The vision is spectacular! "Heaven is open, and I see Jesus!" The last book of the Bible is about Jesus! It is the Revelation of Jesus Christ—the revelation by Jesus, about Jesus. This scene, more than any other in the book, demonstrates this fact. This time the Son of Man, Jesus, appears riding on a white horse. The horse is a symbol of war; this time He appears as a warrior. In the first century when a king rode a horse, he was riding to war. If the king rode a donkey, he was riding to peace. On Palm Sunday, Jesus rode a donkey into the city of Jerusalem, fulfilling the prophecy of Zechariah 9:9–10 (ESV):

> *Rejoice greatly, O daughter of Zion!*
>
> *Shout in triumph, O daughter of Jerusalem!*
>
> *Behold, your king is coming to you;*
>
> *He is just and endowed with salvation,*
>
> *Humble, and mounted on a donkey. . . .*
>
> *And he will speak peace to the nations;*
>
> *And his dominion will be from sea to sea. . . .*

Jesus rode the donkey to accomplish the mission of the cross: to bring peace. The donkey was prepared and waiting beforehand. "As they approached Jerusalem and came to Bethphage and Bethany at the Mount of Olives, Jesus sent two of his disciples, saying to them, 'Go to the village ahead of you, and just as you enter it, you will find a colt [donkey] tied there, which no one has ever ridden. Untie it and bring it here. If anyone asks you, 'Why are you doing this?' say, 'The Lord needs it and will send it back here shortly.' They went and found a colt outside in the street, tied at a doorway. As they untied it, some people standing there asked, 'What are you doing, untying that colt?' They answered as Jesus had told them to, and the people let them go. When they brought the colt to Jesus and threw their cloaks over it, he sat on it."[1]

Just as Jesus had seen Nathanael praying under the fig tree and just as He knew that the rooster would crow three times before Peter denied Him, He knew the donkey would be tied there waiting. The omnipotent, eternal God outside of time, through the power of His word, had ordered all the details and movements, pastures and stables in that little donkey's life for it to be right there at that precise moment for his divine assignment to carry the King. God had also prepared the hearts of the colt's owners.

God had it in His plan before the beginning of time. Since before the serpent slithered and Eve took the bite, Jesus saw and knew the donkey would be waiting. He rode into Jerusalem the perfect Lamb to be sacrificed—the Word made flesh that dwelt among us, on a divine assignment to bring peace between broken mankind and His Creator.

Now, in Revelation 19, Jesus rides on a white horse, for He is riding to war. The Lion/Lamb/Warrior rides to the final battle,

---

1   Mark 11:1–7 NIV

which is never fought because He already fought it on the cross. His robe is already dipped in His own blood. The King of kings and Lord of lords is merely taking possession of what is already His. Jesus is coming for what has been called by many throughout church history "the final battle." And while it is the final showdown, it could be put a more accurate way because "the final battle" to which Jesus rides is actually never fought. It is never fought because it need not be fought. The final battle was the cross when, as the apostle Paul put it, "Having disarmed principalities and powers, He [Jesus] made a public spectacle of them, triumphing over them in it."[2] The "final battle" need not be fought because it has already been fought and won. Jesus Christ rides to finally implement the victory of the cross with His army of redeemed following Him.

In this vision of Jesus, the Warrior, we see that He uses only one weapon, His mouth. "Out of His mouth," writes John, "is a sharp sword with which to strike down the nations. . . The rest were killed with the sword coming out the mouth of the rider on the horse" (Rev. 19:15, 21 NIV). The sword that comes out of His mouth is His word. *Jesus wins simply by speaking.*

This has always been the case. "In the beginning was the Word."[3] He said, "Let there be light," and there was. He said, "Let there be sea monsters," and there were.[4] Out of nothing! He simply spoke into the nothingness, and something came into being. And when the Word became flesh and dwelt among us, He healed the broken and liberated the chained. The demonic shriveled under the power of His command like pawns before their high-ranking military officer.

When the storm raged on the Sea of Galilee, threatening to

---

2   Colossians 2:14–15 NKJV
3   John 1:1 KJV
4   Genesis 1:21 AMP

engulf them, Jesus simply spoke the words, "Hush, be still," and the sea became like glass. At the tomb of Lazarus, Jesus said, "Lazarus, come out!" And the corpse, dead for four days, gasped for breath and stepped forward, his body still wrapped with strips of linen and a cloth around his face. All because of a word, the Word's spoken word.

"I saw heaven standing open." What we have to understand is that heaven is not billions of light years away on another planet in some faraway galaxy. It's not someplace out there amongst the stars. No, heaven is near, all around us, only in another dimension. Bible scholar Robyn Whitaker wrote, "In the biblical tradition . . . heaven is a parallel realm where everything operates according to God's will."[5] Darrell Johnson adds, "The One who rides out of heaven when it is opened is not far away. . . He is very close at hand. At any moment He can break through—that is what 'apocalypse' means. [You can see then that the phrase 'the second coming of Jesus Christ' is not quite accurate. For He is not coming from a distant place. One day He is simply going to pull back the curtain...]"[6] Jesus is going to step, or ride, through the sky much like He stepped through the walls of the house and appeared to the disciples after His resurrection. "I saw heaven standing open." And look! The KING OF KINGS AND LORD OF LORDS! HERE HE COMES!

---

5   https://theconversation.com/what-and-where-is-heaven-the-answers-are-at-the-heart-of-the-easter-story-115451

6   Darrell Johnson, *Discipleship on the Edge: An Expository Journey Through the Book of Revelation* (Vancouver, BC: Canadian Church Leaders Network, 2021), 331

KING OF KINGS AND LORD OF LORDS
David Binion and Mitch Wong

Verse 1
See the Rider, a horse of white
Angel armies, battle lines
There's a fire in Your eyes
As You come riding
As You come riding

Verse 2
On Your head are many crowns
A mighty sword comes from Your mouth
Kingdoms rise, You strike them down
As You come riding
As You come riding

Chorus
King of kings and Lord of lords
The victory is Yours
The victory is Yours
With perfect judgment
You wage war
The victory is Yours
The victory is Yours

Verse 3
You are Faithful, You are True
There is no defying You

Sovereign-Strong You will subdue

As You come riding
As You come riding

BRIDGE
King of kings
Lord of lords
Jesus You will reign forevermore
Hallelujah
Hear us roar
Jesus You will reign forevermore

16

THE WEDDING

Let us rejoice and be glad and give him glory!
For the wedding of the Lamb has come, and his bride has made herself ready.
Fine linen, bright and clean, was given her to wear.
(Fine linen stands for the righteous acts of God's holy people.)
Revelation 19:7–8 NIV

Right before my wife, Nicole, and I got engaged, I purchased her ring in Israel. I had it made special. I chose a ruby and a sapphire to be placed on the sides with an emerald-cut diamond rising up in the middle. It was beautiful. When I returned home, I arranged to take Nicole to downtown Chicago for a date night. We had dinner first, then walked a couple of blocks where I had reserved a horse and carriage. We rode through the streets of one of our favorite cities holding hands. While I had her hand perfectly placed in mine, at just the right angle, I took the ring from my pocket and slid it onto her finger. Her face lit up. She was thrilled! I've always loved her smile, but this was sheer elation. She said yes! And we kissed. There, I said it!

We spent the next year anticipating the wedding day. When? We chose June 11, 1994. The perfect day. Why? Because it was our day. Where? We contemplated having it in a beautiful cathedral somewhere in Chicago but decided not to throw that bill on her mom and dad. So we got married in the church where I was on staff as the worship pastor. Then we had to decide who to invite to be in our bridal party. What about the music? We had to have the best! The ceremony lasted an hour and a half. I think we got carried away. But it was a beautiful night.

We were engaged for a year, but it only felt like a few months. We were in love. We had no doubts about our future together. As I consider this chapter about the impending ceremony between the Groom and the Bride, the church of Jesus Christ, I find myself contemplating my own wedding. As wonderful as it was, it doesn't even compare to what lies ahead for the people of God.

Now let us consider the culture that John was speaking to as he wrote to the seven churches. The process was in some cases the same. The waiting. The anticipating. But there are vast differences as well. In first-century Judaism there were three steps in getting married. First was the engagement, a betrothal; the second was the preparation for the wedding; and then there was the wedding supper itself. John's audience understood these customs. If you and I can understand these steps, we can more fully grasp what is being revealed. Remember, this is the Revelation of Jesus, and His intention is ultimately for His bride.

The marriage process technically began with the betrothal ceremony. The groom-to-be, along with his best man, would leave his father's house and travel to the future bride's house.

There the groom would make arrangements with the father of the bride, basically coming to an agreement on a purchase price. In those days a bride was bought with a price called a dowry. As soon as the groom paid it, the marriage became official even though it would be a period of time before they consummated their union and lived together as husband and wife. This "new" covenant was sealed by drinking a cup of wine. During this betrothal period, which was usually about a year, the bride was considered "set apart" exclusively for the groom.

The groom would then return to his father's house and begin preparing a place for his bride. While this was happening, the bride would prepare herself for the wedding. When the betrothal period was over, the groom, along with his closest friends, would return to the bride's house for her. It was a big, festive moment. The bride and her friends and family knew he was going to come back, just not the precise day or hour. They had to keep themselves ready. This added excitement, anticipation, and an element of mystery to the occasion. I love the prophetic implications here. Quite often, the groom would arrive during the night or wee hours of the morning and would announce with a shout, "The bridegroom is coming! Come out and welcome him!"[1] The bride, consecrated and veiled, with her bridesmaids carrying lamps, would enthusiastically greet the groom and his friends. Let the party begin!

At the bride's feast, there was a brief ceremony involving the word "take." The groom would "take" the bride from her home. This is where the Hebrew expression "take a wife" originated. After the groom "took" his bride, the whole bridal party would travel to the groom's father's house. Wedding guests dressed in special robes would be gathered and waiting. When the bridal party arrived, the feast would take off! The celebration would last seven days, sometimes fourteen.

I can't help but consider that as the seven churches are receiving this message from their pastor, the pain and persecution they have suffered is eclipsed by visions of the day their struggling will end and they'll be received by the Bridegroom, Jesus, into the eternal dance of heaven.

Now consider this: Around A.D. 33, in Jerusalem, Jesus is having the Passover meal with His disciples in an upper room. He

---

1   See Matthew 25:6.

takes a cup of wine, gives it to His disciples, and says, "This cup is the new covenant in my blood."[2] Jesus then tells them He is leaving. What's more, He tells them that they cannot come where He is going.[3] The disciples start freaking out, but Jesus calms them by saying, "Let not your hearts be troubled; believe in God, believe also in me. In my father's house are many dwelling places; if it were not so, I would have told you; for I go to prepare a place for you. And if I go and prepare a place for you, I will come again, and receive you to myself; that where I am, there you may be also."[4]

Do you hear what Jesus is claiming? He is the bridegroom, the husband of the people of God. We are His bride. He has paid the "purchase price" with His own blood. He has sealed the engagement with a cup of wine: "This cup is the new covenant in my blood."[5] Jesus is preparing a place for us in His Father's house, and He is coming to take us to Himself to be His forever!

We have been betrothed!

We are engaged to Jesus Christ!

He paid our price with His own blood! That's how valuable we are. Flawed but incredibly valuable. Do you feel worthless sometimes? I know you've heard it a million times but consider this: The value of something is determined by how much someone is willing to pay for it. Our value must be crazy high because Jesus paid the price needed to buy His bride. We are THAT valuable. You are THAT valuable. Stop letting the world define you by its stupid and vain measurements and trust the One who bought you and married you. He's preparing a place for you too!

Imagine how John's heart must have raced when, as the

---

2   Luke 22:20 NIV
3   John 13:36
4   John 14:1–3 NKJV
5   Luke 22:20 NKJV

Revelation unfolded, he heard the multitude shouting, "Hallelujah! The time has come for the marriage feast!" Send out the invitations. "Blessed is everyone who is invited to the marriage supper of the Lamb."

Look again carefully at our passage from above: "Let us rejoice and be glad and give him glory! For the wedding of the Lamb has come, and his bride has made herself ready. Fine linen, bright and clean, was given her to wear. Fine linen stands for the righteous acts of God's holy people" (Rev. 19:7–8 NIV). There's a bit of contradiction, it seems, in these verses. And we can see it throughout the New Testament. In one verse it says, "The bride has made herself ready." But then the next verse says, "Fine linen, bright and clean, was given her to wear." Which is it? Did she make herself ready or did the Groom give her something that made her ready? Do we prepare ourselves for that day? Or does God do something in us that prepares us for that day? It is the same tension found in Philippians where it says, "Continue to work out your salvation with fear and trembling, for it is God who works in you to will and to act in order to fulfill his good purpose."[6]. Who's doing the work? We disciples? Or Jesus? The answer is "Yes. Both."

Jesus calls us to Himself by grace and then in an intimate relationship with Him we enter the dance, and He begins to free us, especially from our captivity to Babylon, and to empower us to live a new life. Our new life leads to new deeds: "The righteous acts of God's holy people" (Rev. 19:8 NIV). Yet it is because of His presence—the Holy Spirit of Jesus inside us at work in us—that we are able to do the new deeds. "Like a divine dance, our lives shift from performance-based religion and activities to having our eyes locked on Jesus in love, our arms firmly embracing Him in order to

---

6   Philippians 2:12-13 NIV

follow His lead, stepping where He steps, stopping where He stops, fully trusting when He twirls and dips us."[7] The righteous acts or good deeds that we do are not to make us accepted, but because we already are accepted. He makes us ready by enabling us to be ready. It is primarily His work. In Revelation 21:11, John speaks of the bride "having the glory of God." It is having the glory of God that prepares the bride.

Paul told us that "Christ also loved the church and gave Himself for her, that He might sanctify and cleanse her . . ."[8] Or as God says in the tender text in Ezekiel,

"I spread the corner of my garment over you . . .

I bathed you . . .

I anointed you . . .

I clothed you . . .

I wrapped you . . .

I adorned you . . .

I also swore to you and entered into a covenant with you so that you became mine."[9]

Therefore, the multitude cries, "Hallelujah!" The bride (the Church) is ready to enter into the feast, which lasts not seven days or even fourteen days but forever. The eternal dance. What does all of this mean right now, today, tomorrow, and next week? I'm glad you asked! It means at least six things.

1. You are engaged.

If we are engaged to the Lamb, this completely shifts our understanding of the nature of Jesus' love for us.

---

7 Max Davis, *Jesus, Josiah, & Me* (Lake Mary, Florida Charisma Media/Charisma House Book Group, 2021), 131.

8 Ephesians 5:25–26 NKJV

9 Ezekiel 16:8–11, 62 ESV

We are His disciples and His friends, and He loves us! We are His sisters and brothers, and He loves us! We are His temple, the holy place where He dwells, and He loves us! We are His body, and He loves us! All of this would be enough, but the Revelation of Jesus teaches us that our Lord loves us more tenderly, more authentically, more affectionately than all of that. For He loves us as His bride!

I love my children. And I love my parents. And I love my friends and the colleagues with whom I work. I even love my dog. I love how he follows me into every room. He's sitting in the room with me now as I write this. I also love to sing. I love to play the piano. Sometimes I'll just sit and play all by myself. But no one gets loved by me the way my wife does. It's just different! So, understand this: We are Jesus' bride! We are the bride of the Lord of the universe. His love for us is the passionate love of a bridegroom for his bride.

2. It means you are bought with a price.

If we are engaged to the Lamb, then we can be confident and secure. We have been bought with a price: His own blood. We are not our own any longer. We are His! He has brought us into a covenant, which He will never break. Jesus declared, "This is the new covenant in my blood."[10] He will never walk away from us. He will never give up on us. As the lover in the Song of Solomon sings, "My beloved is mine, and I am his."[11] More than that, she sings, "I am my beloved's, and his desire is for me."[12] Our desire for Him, as strong as it is, can never be compared to His desire for us. And nothing can stand in the way of His fulfilling His desire to have us!

3. Loyalty

If we are engaged to the Lamb, then the fundamental issue for us is loyalty, or fidelity. We do not want to be found in bed with

---

10 Luke 22:20 NIV
11 Song of Solomon 2:16 NKJV
12 Song of Solomon 7:10 NIV

another lover. Babylon, the harlot, is powerful and seductive. She has her Jezebels who deceive us into thinking that we can live by the agenda and value system of the harlot while engaged to the Lamb. Just putting it that way makes clear how ridiculous the proposal is. I wrote this song several years ago:

> My heart belongs to You.
>
> My heart belongs to You.
>
> I'll never give myself to another.
>
> My heart belongs to You.

> I used to give away my affection.
>
> Turning my eyes to the things of this world.
>
> Lost in my search for true satisfaction,
>
> Then You came into my world.

> Now that You've gained my deepest affection
>
> I'll never take my eyes off of You.
>
> Cause my heart is filled with anticipation
>
> Of more and more of You.

We cannot be engaged to two brides. People have tried and what a mess they end up in! Never have I felt the issue so deeply. The harlot or the bride? Of course it has to be the bride!

4. Sin is adultery.

If we are engaged to the Lamb, then sin is worse than we thought. Sin is adultery. It is not only missing the mark or stepping over the line or "twistedness." It is adultery. It is profoundly relational. The Old Testament speaks of sin the way it does because Israel has not only wandered away from God, or rebelled against God, as horrible as that is. Israel has committed adultery against her Husband.

In the prophet Jeremiah, after God remembers Israel's first love, and after God asks what He did to Israel that she should go after other lovers, Israel still claims to be loyal. God replies,

"How can you say, 'I am not defiled; I have not run after the Baals'? See how you behaved in the valley; consider what you have done. You are a swift she-camel running here and there, a wild donkey accustomed to the desert, sniffing the wind in her craving— in her heat who can restrain her? Any males that pursue her need not tire themselves; at mating time they will find her."[13]

The word picture is repulsive. But is that not how it is with sin?

"You have scattered your favors . . . under every green tree."[14]

SIN IS ADULTERY.

5. Be ready.

If we are engaged to the Lamb, then the call to loyalty is a call to be ready. The bridegroom has gone away to prepare a room in His Father's house. And oh, what a house it is. I can hardly wait until we get to Revelation 21–22! As He is preparing the room, we are to be preparing ourselves. "The righteous acts of God's holy people." His saints. His bride. All those little acts of loyalty are slowly but surely changing us "from glory to glory."[15] All those sacred moments when we say, "I am Yours, Jesus," are accumulating into even deeper intimacy.

6. The simplicity of intimacy

---

13   Jeremiah 2:23–24 NIV
14   Jeremiah 3:13 NIV
15   2 Corinthians 3:18 NKJV

Finally, if we are engaged to the Lamb, then we must answer the call to simplicity. Our lives are far too busy. And we wonder why we lose intimacy. You who are married, remember when you were engaged? Remember how simple life was? The only thing that mattered was being with her or him. Amazing how it worked. We found all kinds of time. Being in love does that. It simplifies things. The call to discipleship, especially under the pressure of Babylon, is the call to do whatever it takes to stay in love, to live in intimacy with Jesus Christ.

Hallelujah! The marriage of the Lamb has come. And His bride has made herself ready. Blessed is everyone who is invited to the marriage supper of the Lamb!

THE WEDDING

Mitch Wong, Madison Binion, and David Binion

VERSE 1

Oh, what a day it's going to be
When You stand in front of me
And I'll see Your face fully
THE UNVEILING

Oh, to have waited patiently
To be dressed in righteous deeds
To be robed in purity
At the Wedding

CHORUS

I am Your Bride
You are my Groom
You will have me
And I'll have You
We'll drink of the wine
We'll taste of the fruit
The moment we say
I do, I do
We're longing to say
I do, I do

VERSE 2

Oh, it is beautiful indeed
To have loved You faithfully

To be taken as worthy
At the Wedding

BRIDGE
This is divine romance
I'll take Your hand
And we will dance eternally
In this divine romance
Just like we planned
Oh, we will dance eternally

17

ALL THINGS NEW

Now I saw a new heaven and a new earth, for the first heaven and the first earth had passed away. Also there was no more sea. Then I, John, saw the holy city, New Jerusalem, coming down out of heaven from God, prepared as a bride adorned for her husband. And I heard a loud voice from heaven saying, "Behold, the tabernacle of God is with men, and He will dwell with them, and they shall be His people. God Himself will be with them and be their God. And God will wipe away every tear from their eyes; there shall be no more death, nor sorrow, nor crying. There shall be no more pain, for the former things have passed away."

Revelation 21:1-4 NKJV

We live in a society driven by fear. Politicians play on it. Advertisers exploit it. Satan relishes it. Yet throughout Scripture God tells us to "fear not" in one form or another well over a hundred times. But the Book of Revelation rouses fear, some say. With all the wrath and plagues poured out, beasts and dragons, blood and wars, shouldn't we be afraid? If you are, you are either not His or you are viewing the Book of Revelation through the wrong set of lenses. It should be viewed through the lens of grace, not fear. Now, if you are not His, you have a lot to be fearful of, but not if you belong to Him. The Revelation of Jesus is ultimately about grace because He is about grace. As His bride, instead of fearing the future, we look forward to it. Our future is not unknown. God is making all things new. He is redeeming, restoring, and reconciling this fallen, broken world while dealing with evil and righting every wrong. Satan is the "god" of this world for now. "The god of this world has blinded the minds of the unbelievers, to keep them from seeing the light of the gospel of the glory of Christ."[1] Part of that blindness is the glorious future for God's people. When Adam and Eve sinned in the garden, they gave legal right/domain over to Satan to become the dictator of this world, running it with his wicked schemes and principalities and powers and rulers of the darkness of this age, which is the spirit of Babylon.[2] But God is getting it back, legally. His plan has been in place since before the fall. He is remaking our true home.

I know it sounds too good to be true, but it's not wishful thinking. It's a reality. "He has also set eternity in the human heart," wrote Solomon.[3] There's a longing built inside every human being for something more that this world can't completely satisfy. It's a longing for home. C. S. Lewis put it this way, "If we find ourselves with a desire that nothing in this world can satisfy, the most probable explanation is that we were made for another world."[4] Bottom line: Revelation is about Jesus and home. In Revelation 21:1–22:5 we have a crystal-clear snapshot of our future in Jesus—of home. It also reveals the heart of God. There's no need to fear the future if we know Him. "Perfect love casts out fear," wrote John.[5] In the midst of all his persecution and suffering, John knew perfect love. He knew Jesus as the One who died for him on the cross and also the Son of God in heaven.

The message of Revelation is about the end of this age, but it's also about the beginning of a new one. "Now I saw a new heaven and a new earth, for the first heaven and the first earth had passed

---

1   2 Corinthians 4:4 ESV
2   Ephesians 6:12
3   Ecclesiastes 3:11 NIV
4   https://www.goodreads.com/quotes/6439-if-we-find-ourselves-with-a-desire-that-nothing
5   1 John 4:18 NKJV

away" (Rev. 21:1 NKJV). It's about our ultimate home. Everything in this life is preparing us for our final and eternal home, even our gifts. The giftings He gave us on earth, regardless of how small or insignificant they may seem, are going to be utilized to their fullness in heaven— musicians, writers, carpenters, cooks, and horse whisperers. Somehow, God is going to utilize our gifts and bents for His future creations. Creation is not going to stop in heaven. It's only getting started! The God of creation is not going to stop creating. We are going to be involved in some way doing God's work. That's why obedience is so important. We're not going to float around on a cloud for eons. No, we are going to worship and work. Our work will be our worship too. We will live in a perpetual state of His presence with no sin nature to deal with. No lust, greed, envy, fatigue, and brain fog interrupting our flow. Just uninhibited life in His presence. "Then He who sat on the throne said, 'Behold, I make all things new'" (Rev. 21:5 NKJV). Notice God didn't say, "I will make all new things," "but I make all things new." Placement of the word "new" after the word "things" in this sentence is critical. It means God is remaking all things that have *been* made, including us.

People tend to have this limited, religious view of heaven, but we have to put on new glasses that widen our view. "In My Father's house are many mansions; if it were not so, I would have told you. I go to prepare a place for you," said Jesus.[6] Wow! Think of it. God spoke and all of creation came into being, from butterflies to buffaloes, from microscopic tardigrades to supernovas and everything in between. Our mansion may be our own planet or a galaxy. For sure, it's going to be more magnificent and amazing than anything from this world! Stop limiting God to our limited perceptions. In eternity our minds are going to be unleashed. As

6   John 14:2 NKJV

we have seen, currently we understand in part, but then we will understand in full. Everything will be in full. This is the message of the Book of Revelation. A world without sin, a world without limits. The Book of Revelation is the biblical story of time and how it is coming to an end, but the end is actually the beginning of a whole new world outside of time. A child in the womb can't imagine the wonderful, vast, amazing new world waiting outside the confines of the uterus. Likewise, we can't imagine our wonderful, amazing new world awaiting us. Revelation gives us a glimpse.

"And I saw the holy city, new Jerusalem, coming down out of heaven from God, prepared as a bride adorned for her husband" (Rev. 21:2 ESV). Can you see it? The bride coming down the aisle, the city coming down made by God, with Jesus, for us. Home—"I go to prepare a place." You have to read about it! Go ahead. This passage is a bit lengthy, but it's anything but boring.

> *"Come, I will show you the bride, the Lamb's wife." And he carried me away in the Spirit to a great and high mountain, and showed me the great city, the holy Jerusalem, descending out of heaven from God, having the glory of God. Her light was like a most precious stone, like a jasper stone, clear as crystal. Also, she had a great and high wall with twelve gates, and twelve angels at the gates, and names written on them, which are the names of the twelve tribes of the children of Israel: three gates on the east, three gates on the north, three gates on the south, and three gates on the west. Now the wall of the city had twelve foundations, and on them were the names of the twelve apostles of the Lamb. And he who talked with me had a gold reed to measure the city, its gates, and its wall. The city is laid out as a square; its length is as great as its breadth. And he measured the city with the reed: twelve thousand furlongs. Its length, breadth, and height are equal. Then he measured its wall: one hundred and forty-four cubits, according to the measure of a man, that is, of an angel. The construction of its*

wall was of jasper; and the city was pure gold, like clear glass. The foundations of the wall of the city were adorned with all kinds of precious stones: the first foundation was jasper, the second sapphire, the third chalcedony, the fourth emerald, the fifth sardonyx, the sixth sardius, the seventh chrysolite, the eighth beryl, the ninth topaz, the tenth chrysoprase, the eleventh jacinth, and the twelfth amethyst. The twelve gates were twelve pearls: each individual gate was of one pearl. And the street of the city was pure gold, like transparent glass (Rev. 21:9–21 NKJV).

I don't know about you, but I don't want to miss heaven! My brain is about to explode. I want to stop and just worship. Heaven and the New Jerusalem are literal places. They are not metaphors. After Jesus rose from the dead, He ate with the disciples. They felt His hands and touched Him. He had a glorified body. So will we. It's hard to wrap our minds around it, but those stones in the New Jerusalem will be just as real as this book in your hands. And we are being drawn to our new home every day because home is planted in our hearts. When we understand Revelation in this way, our perspective changes.

It's grace. Heaven is the fulfillment of God's grace. It's His gift to us. Of course, the Book of Revelation is about judgment of sin and evil, but it's ultimately about God's grace—the Revelation of Jesus, who is the fullest manifestation of grace. He took the wrath of God for us, bought us, and paid the dowry. We are His, but the world has to be made right and justice served. It's about us, but it's about so much more than us. Principalities and powers were defeated, brought to justice, and the universe brought back into alignment. Drop one tiny speck of something unclean into a pure glass of drinking water and it is contaminated. To get it pure again, it has to be taken through a process of filtration. God cannot allow sin to contaminate heaven the way it did this earth. This is the message of Revelation. All things made new. All things purified. A new heaven, a new Jerusalem, a new earth. "Then He who sat on the throne said, 'Behold, I make all things *new*.' And He said to me, 'Write, for these words are true and faithful.' And He said to me, 'It is done! I am the Alpha and the Omega, the Beginning and the End. I will give of the fountain of the water of life freely to him who thirsts'" (Rev. 21:5–6 NKJV, emphasis added).

Tears and pain will be gone too. "And God will wipe away every tear from their eyes; there shall be no more death, nor sorrow, nor crying. There shall be no more pain, for the former things have passed away" (Rev. 21:4 NKJV). Can you imagine no death? People talk about the great circle of life as if death is a natural process and should be embraced, kumbaya. No. Death is a curse. We were not created to die. We were created to live eternally. Trust me, watching your parents age is no fun. Of course, we can live out our days fully. That is God's best. But our bodies will age, and we will die. The Psalmist wrote, "So teach us to number our days, that we may gain a heart of wisdom."[7] Wisdom is understanding that our time on earth is short, that life is a vapor. The Book of Revelation shows us this world is temporal and our ultimate home is eternal. Understanding Revelation gives us an eternal perspective on suffering too. When heaven is our home, our worst day on earth is our best day. "O death, where is your sting?"[8]

Revelation 21:8 continues, "But the cowardly, unbelieving, abominable, murderers, sexually immoral, sorcerers, idolaters, and all liars shall have their part in the lake which burns with fire and brimstone, which is the second death" (NKJV). Ouch! Babylon can't enter heaven. Our sin nature has to be dealt with before we

---

7   Psalm 90:12 NKJV
8   1 Corinthians 15:55 NKJV

can enter. We must be born anew.[9] Sin is why we die physically and spiritually. Those born again by the Spirit of God and washed clean by the blood of the Lamb are alive spiritually, but their physical bodies are still decaying. One day our physical bodies will catch up with our spirits. "So when this corruptible has put on incorruption, and this mortal has put on immortality, then shall be brought to pass the saying that is written: 'Death is swallowed up in victory.'"[10] That speck of dirt can't contaminate the pure. Those armies dressed in fine white linen in heaven are washed clean, purified by the Lamb.

But grace. "For the wages of sin is death, but the gift of God is eternal life in Christ Jesus our Lord."[11] If you want eternal life in heaven, receive His free gift. The wrath of God is upon those who reject His free gift through unbelief.[12] Riding on the white horse was the One called Faithful and True. "He who overcomes shall inherit all things, and I will be his God and he shall be My son" (Rev. 21:7 NKJV). Overcoming is all about clinging to His promises. "Let us hold unswervingly to the hope we profess, for he who promised is faithful."[13] We can trust in His promises because He is faithful and true.

"But I saw no temple in it, for the Lord God Almighty and the Lamb are its temple" (Rev. 21:22 NKJV).[14] We will live in His presence. "In Your presence is fullness of joy; at Your right hand are pleasures forevermore."[15] Living in His presence will be a life full of peace and joy unmatched by anything on earth—that feeling my friend Max had worshiping between and along with the two olive trees, that I had while worshiping in the swirl and rush of water.

---

9   John 3:3
10   1 Corinthians 15:54 NKJV
11   Romans 6:23 NKJV
12   John 3:36, Romans 1:15–32
13   Hebrews 10:23 NIV
14   Revelation 21:22 NKJV
15   Psalm 16:11 NKJV

"The city had no need of the sun or of the moon to shine in it, for the glory of God illuminated it. The Lamb is its light" (Rev. 21:23 NKJV). No shadows. I heard the testimony of a man who died and went to heaven. It was incredible, and well-documented. He said in heaven there were no shadows. We don't think it's that big a deal here, but when you live with no shadows it makes an amazing difference. Everything has the glow of the light of God. Not too much, not too little, just perfect. Again, our finite minds can only speculate.

This light will be everywhere. God dwells everywhere. Colors will be more vivid than we can imagine. Maybe new colors. Try to think of a new primary color, not one that is a mixture. You can't do it. It will turn your mind to mush.

A city of light. "Behold, the tabernacle of God is with men, and He will dwell with them, and they shall be His people. God Himself will be with them and be their God. . . . Behold, I make all things new" (Rev. 21:3, 5 NKJV).

ALL THINGS NEW
Mitch Wong, David Binion, Steffany Gretzinger, Gracie Binion

Chorus
All things
You are Making
All things
All things new

Verse 1
Out of heaven, from Your presence
Like a bride prepared for wedding
Holy city, New Jerusalem
You will come and tabernacle
Dwell among Your holy people
Every elder, saint, and seraphim

Chorus
No more wounds
No more pain
Every tear
Wiped away

None will weep
None will mourn
Death is dead
Old is gone

18

EDEN RESTORED

Then the angel showed me the river of the water of life, as clear as crystal,
flowing from the throne of God and of the Lamb down the middle of the great
street of the city. On each side of the river stood the tree of life, bearing twelve
crops of fruit, yielding its fruit every month. And the leaves of the tree are for the
healing of the nations. No longer will there be any curse. The throne of God and
of the Lamb will be in the city, and his servants will serve him.
They will see his face, and his name will be on their foreheads.
There will be no more night. They will not need the light of a lamp or the light
of the sun, for the Lord God will give them light.
And they will reign for ever and ever.

Revelation 22:1–5 NIV

Eden restored. A place of fellowship where God walked with man. Before the fall, Adam walked with God in His continual presence. When that fellowship was broken, everything changed. The curse came and shame entered. Suddenly, Adam and Eve understood they were naked. Or was it that the presence of God had been their covering and when it lifted, they suddenly saw themselves as they were? They tried to cover themselves and hide. Man has been doing that ever since. "Who told you that you were naked?" asked God.[1] Sin exposes us and makes us want to hide. Not anymore. At the end of Revelation, fellowship is fully restored, Eden is restored.

---

1   Genesis 3:11 NIV

BLIND BEFORE I SAW THE GLORY OF EDEN

This story I'm about to share has everything to do with Eden restored. It all started with a dream. Actually, it was a series of dreams that awakened a desire in me to explore the deeper places of God that can only be found in His glory.

In December of 2017, I developed a corneal ulcer in my left eye. The first indication that there was a problem was at a Christmas production in central Florida. This particular night I was seated in the audience waiting for our time to enter the stage and perform the few songs that we were participating in. I was having difficulty with the brightness of the stage lights. I found myself squinting through most of that performance. The next morning as we were walking through the security line at the airport, my daughter noticed a blister forming on my cornea. Coincidentally, we had our annual appointment already scheduled with our eye doctor when we got home that afternoon. The doctor was dumbfounded by the size of the ulcer that was developing on my eye. He said he hadn't seen anything like it in his twenty-five years of practice. He immediately called a specialist in Dallas and arranged for me to go straight to his office. This was the beginning of a six-week process that took my vision. I went blind in that eye.

The specialist put me on a series of medicated eye drops to see if we could arrest the ulcer. I would have to see him every couple of days to monitor the progress. The ulcer eventually became an open sore that grew almost unbearable. Over the next couple of weeks, I would be put on a schedule of medicated eye drops every hour of the day. Six different kinds of drops were prescribed. I had to set an alarm every hour of the night to get up and use the drops. Every drop caused horrible pain. As the weeks progressed, I was unable to stand any kind of light in my eyes. On Christmas Day I found myself in a dark bedroom because it was too painful to sit at the dinner table with the family under the lights in the dining room. After six weeks of dark sunglasses with extra light blockers placed behind each lens, the doctor told me that I would lose the eye completely if I didn't get a cornea transplant. I had been praying for a miracle. Remember, I grew up around the miraculous. I witnessed countless miracles as a young man traveling with my parents in healing revivals. I started experiencing even more of the miraculous in our own services as we led worship in services around the nation. People would just get healed while we worshiped. So, my expectation was that God would heal me. But the healing didn't come, and I was faced with this decision. Nicole and I agreed that I would have the surgery.

The first night home after the surgery, with the patch still covering my eye, uncertain of the outcome, I went to sleep and fell into a series of dreams. I know that I was in the presence of God, but I have never seen this before. I was fully aware that I was in a presence place, but it was uncharted territory for me. It was almost like cutting through a beautiful jungle with a machete, except there was no machete. The leaves of the bushes would just unfold and let me through. At some point I was led out into an opening and there was some kind of indiscernible form that came out with me, like an angelic guide. I remember feeling like I needed to get the thing back to where it came from before someone caught me. This was an unusual detail, but it's how I felt in the dream. And then before I could return it, I would wake up.

Strangely, when I awoke, I couldn't remember what I had just dreamed. I only remember being frustrated. I dreamed the episode several times. And each time I'd wake up frustrated that I was unable to remember the dream. Finally, I was having the dream for the last time, and I was now narrating to myself what was about to happen. I was going through this uncharted presence place filled with beautiful greenery. I remember saying to myself in the dream, "This is where you'll come out into the open, and the form, whatever it is, will be there with you."

Then suddenly I was shaken out of my sleep by a deep voice that said, "The glory of Eden has broken through!" I jolted up into a sitting position, stunned by the voice. The glory of Eden? I wasn't even sure what that meant. But I was no longer uncomfortable in its presence. Instead, I became intrigued and started staring into it, trying to behold it, but it wasn't physically visible. I didn't know what the glory of Eden was, but I liked the sound of it. I realized that I was awake but still in some kind of vision. I saw a girl standing maybe fifteen feet away who was wounded and broken from years of abuse and pain. My instinct was to will the "glory of Eden" to move toward her. I didn't say a word, I just wanted her to experience it. As I released it toward her, I felt the rush of heaven blow from behind me in her direction, and instantly she was healed and whole. At that moment, I reached my hand behind me into the presence place, and I became aware of a room filled with orphaned miracles looking for a home. I pulled my hand back and in my hand was the answer for cancer, and I instinctively released it as the rush of heaven came blowing past me again.

Somehow, I fell back into a peaceful sleep the rest of the night. When I awoke the next morning, my head began to swim with thoughts of Eden and what it all meant. I removed the patch from my eye, able to see clearly with no pain! I was grateful to the Lord. The next several nights I continued to have these extraordinary dreams. I wasn't sure what was happening, but I was thrilled!

At this point I need to explain what happens with cornea surgeries. Basically, my replacement cornea came from someone who had died and donated their body to science. The cornea from a person who was dead was now alive, fully functioning in me. I call that resurrected vision. I didn't get the miracle that I asked for, but instead I started having divine dreams.

A few nights later I woke up around 2:00 a.m. (I checked the clock), and for three hours all I could see was a line from a song I had written: "There is a swirling of glory on the face of the deep once again. . ." I could literally see the image of the "face" of the Spirit, moving through the darkness. The twinkle of revelation was in His eyes, not intimidated in the least by the darkness. Then He said, "Let there be light," and there was no contest: The darkness was obliterated! Blazing light! The line from this song rolled over and over, and it was as if I was seeing it for the first time, before Eden.

> There is a swirling of glory on the face of the deep once again.
>
> And then I see our world right now. Seemingly darker than it's ever been.
>
> And I behold a sea of faces. Heads lifted. And the swirling . . .
>
> When He comes to your face, what will He find?
>
> A surrendered heart, or a contender, fighting for your place in the light?
>
> On your mountain, in your sphere of influence?
>
> Narcissistic? Or surrendered?
>
> Let there be! Then the kingdom comes! The kingdoms of this world become something else. Is this past or present? Or just "IS"? Always. Eternal.
>
> There is a swirling on the face of the deep once again. Lift up your heads, oh ye gates.
>
> Lift up your face and behold His!

For context, here are the lyrics that I wrote with Reba Rambo about fifteen years ago.

Could this be the gateway of heaven?

Could this be the doorway of grace?

Is the King of the Ages among us?

Is the Lord really here in this place?

Cause there is a signature fragrance

And the sound of abundance of rain

There is a swirling of glory

On the face of the deep once again

The angels dance up, down the ladder

Announcing the birth of His word

And all of creation is trembling

As the cry of redemption is heard

And the kingdom of heaven kisses the earth

The spell of the darkness is broken

The world is embraced by the Prince of the Light

The dreams that were dead have awoken

The Daystar of Hope is arising to shine

And He sings of the dawning of freedom

The song of the Lamb, and the Sovereign I am

Is the sound of His heavenly kingdom

Kissing the earth

This vision had happened several nights in a row, replaying
over and over again. I could see the face of the Holy Spirit, a strong
chiseled face, emerging through a dark swirling cloud as it hovered

over a sea of faces.

Now, let's consider Eden. The glory of Eden has broken through. My imagination allows me to consider it all. My first thoughts are the sound of His voice as He declares, "Let there be!" And there was! The grass grew; the trees reached tall as their branches stretched out like arms waking up in the morning light. "Let there be" and the dogs started barking. The cows started mooing. The birds sang their very first song. "Let there be" and there was. The waves of the ocean splashed against the rocks on the shore. A beautiful garden of flowers blossomed for the first time. But then something unusual happens. The same One speaking to the elements as if painting on a canvas pauses and finds a place near the river's edge where the soil is moist. He kneels down and starts shaping something in the dirt. All of the animals look on in wonder, and all of the angels are witnessing it from the other realm. As His hands shape and form the figure, the heavenly beings are whispering to one another, "What is it? What is it?"

Then He leans over and breathes on the form. Eyes start to flutter. Perhaps a cough or a sneeze as the being takes his first breath. Then he sits up and looks around. The angels gasp! "It looks like Him!" His image! Then God places him in a garden and gives him a helpmate, and the story begins.

Here's another song that I wrote with my wife, Nicole, Michael Farren, and Krissy Nordhoff about this series of dreams and visions:

GLORY OF EDEN
David Binion, Nicole Binion, Michael Farren,
Krissy Nordhoff

Verse 1
Once in a garden
Heaven kissed earth
As God breathed His fullness
Into the dirt
The gasp of the angels
"It looks just like Him"
As God started walking
With dust as His friend

Verse 2
Once in a garden
With one whispered lie
Friendship was shattered
And darkness would rise
God could have left it
And called it the end
But He is restoring
The garden again

Chorus
Feel the rush of heaven
Hear the song and the sound
There's no end to the wonder
Here as the glory

The glory of Eden breaks out.

VERSE 3

Nothing can stop it
Once it begins
Hell and the darkness
Have no defense
Rolling like thunder
It's crashing in
God is restoring
The garden again

BRIDGE

See the lame dancing
Their very first dance
The blind stand beholding
The face of the Lamb
The hopeless are singing
The orphans are home
In the glory of Eden
Where we all belong

How does all this relate to the Book of Revelation, or in this case, the Revelation of Jesus? *Eden Restored* started in a garden, and it will ultimately end in a garden. God told Adam to subdue and take dominion in the garden. This was His original plan. "And God blessed them; and God said to them, 'Be fruitful and multiply, and fill the earth, and have dominion. . . .'"[2] God's mandate from the beginning was for Adam to expand the influence of Eden and take dominion of the whole earth. Of course, we know the rest of the story. The serpent slithered in, and Adam sinned and was banished from the garden.

But God already had a plan of redemption in motion. Almost four thousand years later, Jesus prayed so fervently in another garden that His sweat was like great drops of blood. He was setting the stage for redemption and the ultimate restoration of God's original desire. I wonder if Jesus thought about Eden as He prayed in that garden. Ultimately, this is what I've come to believe. Revival is the ordinary Kingdom life. Revival is the atmosphere of heaven. It's proof of heaven on earth. The evidence of Eden. I believe in expanding Eden in the earth and I'm consumed with hunger for MORE! Obviously, Eden will be fully restored when at the end of Revelation God makes all things new. However, with the Holy Spirit of Jesus inside us we can begin the process now, by carrying His presence into all of our situations and as salt and light affecting our environments for Godly change.

---

2   Genesis 1:28 NKJV

EDEN RESTORED

David Binion, Mitch Wong, Steffany Gretzinger,
Madison Grace Binion

VERSE 1

Water clear as crystal
Running from Your throne
Flowing in the middle
Of the City of God
Shimmering
So brilliantly

Drinking from the River
Planted on each side
In the soil of heaven
Lives the tree of life
Soothing leaves
Bring healing

CHORUS

Throughout the ages
Your heart was aching
Anticipating
So long You've waited
You've been so patient
It wasn't wasted

VERSE 2

Every curse is broken

Every face will shine
Welcome back to Eden
No one is denied
Your glory, so holy

Echoing the sound of
Oneness evermore
Footsteps in the garden
Walking with You, Lord
Just like we dreamed
Eternally

BRIDGE
You will have
Your reward
You will see
Eden Restored

19

SOON

He who testifies to these things says, "Yes, I am coming soon."Amen.
Come, Lord Jesus.
The grace of the Lord Jesus be with God's people. Amen.

Revelation 22:20–21 NIV

The Book of Revelation starts with the words "The Revelation of Jesus Christ" and ends with "The grace of the Lord Jesus . . ." As we've seen, if you are His child, the Book of Revelation is not a book of fear but of grace. It's God's ultimate plan of redemption, renewal, and reward for "God's people." Revelation is also a book about worship because, the truth is, until we have realized the depth of our depravity, both personally and as a species, and understand the depth of who Jesus really is and what He has done for us, we can't fully worship. But once the light bulb clicks on, worship can't help itself! It explodes out of our hearts. "Amazing grace, how sweet the sound, that saved a wretch like me. I once was lost, but now am found. Was blind but now I see." If deep gratitude and praise do not well up, I would have to say you don't have a full understanding of your lostness without Him and His amazing provision of grace.

We've come full circle. A lot has happened. In the story of the Bible, the story of redemption, the story of judgment, woven all the way through is Jesus, the Son of Man, the Faithful and True rider, the King of kings and Lord of lords. The story of the whole Bible from Genesis to Revelation is the story of Jesus. He shows up in every book of the Bible. In Genesis He is the Creator and promised

Redeemer. In Exodus, He is our Passover Lamb. In Leviticus He is our High Priest. It goes on through every book of the Bible. In John, He is the Messiah who is the Word, God in the flesh. In Colossians, He is the exact image and representation of God. Finally, in Revelation, He is King of kings and Lord of lords, the Alpha and the Omega, the Beginning and the End. He is coming again. He is the One who makes all things new and is coming again for His bride. "Yes, I am coming soon. . . Amen. Come, Lord Jesus."

When considering the message of Revelation and Jesus coming soon, keep in mind that, as we have discussed prior, time is irrelevant to God. He is outside of time. That half hour of silence in heaven was from John's perspective. Around the Throne, time doesn't exist as it does in our dimension. After the apostle Peter wrote that one day with the Lord is like a thousand years, he continued in the next verse, "The Lord is not slack concerning His promise, as some count slackness, but is longsuffering toward us, not willing that any should perish but that all should come to repentance."[1] Keep in mind, Peter wrote this knowing his martyrdom was imminent.

We start to wonder when, Lord, when? We grow tired and weary, as does the world. The scoffers sneer, "Where is the promise of His coming? For since the fathers fell asleep, all things continue as they were from the beginning of creation."[2] Oh, He is coming, soon. As the leaves rustling in the wind let us know a change in season is coming, we, the people of God, can feel it. The Holy Spirit inside us is leaping like baby John leapt inside Elizabeth's womb when pregnant Mary walked in. We long for that something more, our home, to experience the freedom and joy and wonder of the new world. Mostly, though, we long to see Him face to face. "But we know that when He is revealed, we shall be like Him, for we shall

---

1   2 Peter 3:9 NKJV
2   2 Peter 3:4 NKJV

see Him as He is."[3] The Book of Revelation is that revealing. "And they shall see his face; and his name shall be in their foreheads" (Rev. 22:4 NKJV). Oh, to embrace Him and cling to His feet, kissing them with the tears of our joy and basking in the oil of His love. This. For we shall at last be all that we were created to be, free from our sin nature and "like Him." In the meantime, we occupy. We do our assignments with joy and fulfilment. We wait expectantly for our Groom to come and take us to the place prepared for us. We can clearly see that the world is aging, running its course, that the whole creation is groaning for the day that it "will be delivered from the bondage of corruption into the glorious liberty of the children of God."[4] Revelation is about that deliverance from bondage.

"I am the Alpha and the Omega, the Beginning and the End, the First and the Last"

(Rev. 22:13).

"Yes, I am coming soon" (Rev. 22:20).

---

3   I John 3:2 NKJV
4   Romans 8:21 NKJV

SOON
Mitch Wong, Madison Binion, Abbie Gamboa,
and David Binion

VERSE 1
Trim your lamps and keep them burning
Stay awake for His returning
He's on His way
Hear Him say?

CHORUS
Look I'm coming soon
Look I'm coming soon
Yes, I'm coming soon
Soon soon soon soon

VERSE 2
No one knows the day or timing
Stay alert for His arriving
And don't forget
What He said

BRIDGE
All who are thirsty inside
Who crave for the water of life
Join in the duet divine
The song of the Spirit and the Bride

Come, Lord Jesus

Come, Lord Jesus, come
Come, come quickly
Come, come

David Binion is a Dallas, Texas-based Pastor, and worship leader with a passion to worship God and lead others into His presence. Married for 28 years, David and his wife Nicole have been in ministry together for almost as long, working with a myriad of artists, evangelists, and organizations representing the global church.

Most recently, David and Nicole served as worship pastors for the multi-campus Covenant Church in Texas. After a decade with their Covenant family, the couple stepped away in 2017 to pursue a long-held dream, launching Dwell Ministries to mentor and train a new generation of worshipers, worship leaders, and church creatives. Then in 2018 they started Dwell Church and serve as Lead Pastors.

The Binions, who serve as guest hosts for TBN's flagship "Praise!" program, have also been busy hosting "Dwell Nights" of worship across the U.S. and abroad while planting Dwell Church in Dallas. David and Nicole are signed to Integrity Music and have released several albums, appropriately titled Dwell, in August 2018, Dwell Christmas in 2019, and The Glory Of Eden in 2020.

Max Davis has authored or collaborated on over 35 published books. He has been featured in *USA Today, Publisher's Weekly*, and *Southern Living*, as well as on *BibleGateway*, the *Today* show, *It's Supernatural*, and *The 700 Club*. Max holds degrees in journalism and theology and is a faith-energizing speaker for churches and organizations. God is using Max's hope-infused stories combined with journalistic research and solid biblical teaching to challenge unbelievers, encourage those struggling in their faith, and spark prayer revivals in hearts around the world. In addition to his own works, he's becoming known as one of Christian publishing's top collaborators with highly-notable leaders. Max has a passion for God stories and helping those with a needed message get it out. He lives in south Louisiana under an umbrella of oaks with his wife and best friend, Alanna. To find out more about Max and his books visit www.MaxDavisBooks.com or Google Max Davis author.

Facebook.com/maxdavisauthor

9 781685 565206